LITERATURE IN IRELAND

KENNIKAT PRESS SCHOLARLY REPRINTS
Ralph Adams Brown, Senior Editor

Series In
IRISH HISTORY AND CULTURE
Under the General Editorial Supervision of
Gilbert A. Cahill
Professor of History, State University of New York

LITERATURE IN IRELAND

STUDIES
IRISH AND ANGLO-IRISH

BY

THOMAS MacDONAGH, M.A.
UNIVERSITY COLLEGE, DUBLIN

KENNIKAT PRESS
Port Washington, N. Y./London

LITERATURE IN IRELAND

First published in 1916
Reissued in 1970 by Kennikat Press
Library of Congress Catalog Card No: 79-102612
SBN 8046-0789-3

Manufactured by Taylor Publishing Company   Dallas, Texas

KENNIKAT SERIES IN IRISH HISTORY AND CULTURE

TO

GEORGE SIGERSON

PATRIOT AND SAGE, BARD OF THE GAEL AND GALL,
TEACHER AND HEALER, OLLAMH OF SUBTLE LORE,
WHOSE WORDS AND WORKS TO IRELAND'S PAST RESTORE
THE GLORY THAT WAS LOST WITH LEARNING'S FALL
IN OUR DARK PASSION, THE IMMEMORIAL
KIND KNOWLEDGE WEARS TO US THE MIEN SHE WORE
TO YOUR YOUNG GAZE ; AND, MASTER, LOOK BEFORE,
SEE WHERE THE CHILDREN WEAVE HER CORONAL.

YOUR HONOUR IS YOUR COUNTRY'S : STILL YOU GIVE
YOUR LIFE'S GREAT SERVICE UNDER GOD TO HER,
AND SHE REPAYS IN FULL, EARLY OR LATE.
SO, THAT SOME WORD OF MINE A WHILE MAY LIVE,
SET WITH YOUR NAME IN HER LOVE'S REGISTER,
THESE TO YOU I INSCRIBE AND DEDICATE.

PREFACE.

THESE Studies in Irish and Anglo-Irish Literature are frankly experimental. In them I have tried to clear away certain misconceptions, to fix certain standards, to define certain terms. I trust that as a result the Irish Mode will be better understood and appreciated than the Celtic Note for which I substitute it.

My exclusion from the scope of these inquiries of the Hiberno-English writers of the eighteenth century has already provoked protests from my friends. They do indeed form a band apart in English Literature, with the common characteristic of adventurous and haughty individualism. But to me, who look rather from the Gaelic stand-point, the attitude of Swift, Steele, Sheridan, Burke, Goldsmith and the rest, for all that they have in common and for all that they owe to their Irish birth or upbringing, is an attitude rather of dissent from an English orthodoxy than of consent in an orthodoxy of their own or of Ireland's. Æ has claimed, in conversation with me about this, that all these emigrants, down to Oscar Wilde and Shaw, have that Irish mien of aristocracy that marked our great in the days of the clan system—an aristocracy not of the talents merely, but of character, of self-confident and often self-made leadership. I would not deny their claim. I would not abate their praise. But the two literatures of my choice here have other claims and are worthy of other praise. If I have done a little wrong to the emigrants in one of my Studies, this will undo it.

My subject is Literature in Ireland. My business as regards Gaelic is simple—to show the value of the old literature, the prospects of the new. To this business I have devoted the last and longest of these Studies and portions of others. My theses as regards Anglo-Irish are these three, restated in Study V and dealt with in detail in the rest of the book:—

That an Anglo-Irish literature, worthy of a special designation, could come only when English had become the language of the Irish people, mainly of Gaelic stock, and when the literature was from, by, of, to and for the Irish people.

That the ways of life and the ways of thought of the Irish people—the manners, customs, traditions and outlook, religious, social and moral—have important differences from the ways of life and of thought which have found expression in other English literature.

That the English language in Ireland has an individuality

of its own, and the rhythm of Irish speech a distinct character.

To illustrate my text I have put together at the end a selection of poems in English, examples of the Irish Mode,—poems which show in their form the influence of Gaelic versification, of Irish music or of the Irish way of speech. In my introductory note to these I explain the limitations of the selection.

I have throughout used italics in printing words and quotations from other languages than English. I have, however, used Gaelic type for quotations from modern Irish. For other explanations of this nature I refer readers to the notes at the end.

It is well to let it be known that some of the studies were written before the summer of 1914. The present European wars have altered our outlook on many things, but as they have not altered the truth or the probability of what I have written here, I have not altered my words. As will be seen, I anticipated turbulence and change in the arts. These wars and their sequel may turn literature definitely into ways towards which I looked, confirming the promise of our high destiny here

UNIVERSITY COLLEGE, DUBLIN
    January, 1916.

CONTENTS.

xi

POEMS OF THE IRISH MODE.

CONTENTS.

LITERARY INTRODUCTION.

By Padraic Colum.

These studies, written after the writer's life had been committed to a cause, carry something more than literary knowledge and a literary doctrine : they have personality and a prophetic outlook. "Literature in Ireland" is Thomas MacDonagh's testament : by it he leaves to the Irish generations his knowledge and his discoveries, and, above all, his proud hopes for the resurgent Ireland that he knew. It is one of the few proud books that have been written for us : Thomas MacDonagh, scholar and critic, has taken Ireland for granted : he decries nothing, dispraises nothing, denies nothing of what another people possesses : he has full knowledge of Ireland's achievement in literature and he says "it is good," he has full belief in her destiny and he says "it is brave." And his has been the privilege of adding to Ireland's vision and Ireland's will.

He would, I believe, have dealt fully with novels and stories, with plays and essays in subsequent volumes. In "Literature in Ireland" he deals mainly with Irish

poetry. But although he has applied it to only one
branch—to poetry—he has made a standard by which
we can judge what is typical in our literature.

That racial, that typical expression is not due to a single
quality and it has nothing to do with the abracadabra
that amateurs have drawn out of translations of Celtic
literature : it comes from what psychologists would
speak of as " the national complex "—ideals, traditions,
mentality, the sound of Gaelic poetry and Gaelic music,
the word position of Gaelic speech. MacDonagh sweeps
away the vague " Celtic note " and substitutes a definite
term " The Irish Mode." The lyrics he has selected as
illustrating the Irish mode make the briefest and the
most distinctive anthology of Irish verse in English.

The distinctiveness of the poems he has selected (they
are not all of the poems he might have selected had he,
unhampered by copyrights, wished to make a real anthology) is due primarily to the rhythms. He says truly
that the rhythm of a poem is as representative of the
poet's mind as the words he fixes into it. And the
peculiar rhythms of the poems he has singled out flow
from the influences of Irish versification, Irish speech
and Irish music.

These typical rhythms are not the only expressions of
our national distinctiveness in poetry. MacDonagh
lays a good deal of stress on the exhibition of a certain

naiveté " An Irish poet, if he be individual, if he be
original, if he be national, speaks, almost stammers, one
of the two fresh languages of this country—in Irish
(modern Irish, newly schooled by Europe) or in Anglo-
Irish, English as we speak it in Ireland. . . . Such an
Irish poet can still express himself in the simplest terms
of life and of the common furniture of life." One would
liked to have discussed with him, whether such poetry
as is in the lines he quotes—

> She carries in the dishes
> And lays them in a row—

does not come out of certain social conditions—conditions
that permit of but few possessions. Poetry that celebrates
" the common furniture of life " is in all folk verse and
folk stories. Maeterlinck has imitated it in " The Blue
Bird " when he makes the cat and the dog, water and
sugar creatures in his action. To children brought up
in peasant cottages, in Ireland or elsewhere in Europe,
a clock, a pitcher, a pail of water, a crock of milk, a crack
in a rafter, may gather round themselves imaginative
associations. Such things are not, as they are amongst
people who have many possessions, replaceable, shifting
objects ; they belong to the furniture of the world, like the
sun or the moon. James Stephens has the poetry of " the
common furniture of life " in the story of his that deals

with what might be called the folk-life of Dublin—" The
Charwoman's Daughter." Perhaps poetry with this
sort of content is only distinctive in contrast with the
literature of a people who live through different social
and economic conditions.

It is hard to believe that he who wrote these eloquent,
brave and learned pages is no longer in existence. Those
who saw Thomas MacDonagh in his university robe
and noted his flow of speech and his tendency to
abstractions might have carried away an image of one of
those adventurous students who disputed endlessly in a
medieval university. But MacDonagh was far from
being a pedant—he was a wonderfully good comrade,
an eager friend, a happy-hearted companion. He had
abundance of good spirits and a flow of wit and humour
remarkable even in a Munster man. He had too an inti-
mate knowledge of the humours of popular life in the
country and the country town—a knowledge which he
seldom put into his writing, but which has become vivid
in that unique poem " John-John." His mother was
born in Dublin and was of English parentage, and his
maternal grandfather was, if I remember aright what he
told me, a printer in Trinity College. His mother, at
the time I knew her, had the simplicity, the outlook, the
manner, of a fine type of Irish countrywoman. She and
her husband were teachers in a primary school in

Cloughjordan in Tipperary. Thomas was trained by a religious order and was indeed a religious novice in his youth. He became a teacher in a College in Kilkenny and afterwards in Fermoy. While he was in Kilkenny he took up the study of Irish and he became one of the advance guard of the Gaelic League. In the Arran Islands and in the Irish-speaking districts of Munster he made himself fluent in the language. In 1901 and 1902 he published a volume of literary verse, "Through the Ivory Gate" and "April and May." He had dedicated one of the volumes to Mr. Yeats and had corresponded with him, but he was not then known in the literary groups in Dublin.

I came to know him in 1909 at the time he was teaching in Fermoy. His great interest then was poetry. He knew poetry well in English, French, Latin and Irish, and was drawn to the classical poets—to Horace, to Dante, to Lamartine. The poetry he was writing then was perhaps too literary. After he came to live in Dublin —in 1910—the poetry he wrote was more personal. What he wrote after four years of residence there is in " Songs of Myself."

He came to Dublin with a play which he was anxious to have produced in the Abbey Theatre, which was then under the brief direction of J. M. Synge. The play was " When the Dawn is Come." The scene is laid in a

revolutionary Ireland of the future and the tragedy is
that of a leader whose master-idea baffles his followers.
He wanted to write a play about Owen Roe O'Neill and
another about one of the Gracchi.   In the life of Owen
Roe and in the life of Tiberius or Caius Gracchus there
was the drama that appealed to him—the thoughtful
man become revolutionist and dominating the crowd
for a great end—he saw great drama in the preparation
of the people, in the fierce conflict and the catastrophe.
Many things that Thomas MacDonagh said and wrote
were extraordinarily prophetic—even fatalistic. None
of his utterances were more prophetic than the
play he had produced and the two plays he projected.

His connection with St. Enda's School is well-known
and this part of his career need not be elaborated. He
had been on the staff of the school four years when
"Songs of Myself" was published.   He then went to
Paris to do some reading.   When he returned he took
a degree in the National University.   Professor Houston
of the College of Science, with MacDonagh, James
Stephens and myself started the "Irish Review."
MacDonagh was associate editor, first with the three of
us and, after an interregnum, when there was a single
editor, with his friend Joseph Plunkett. He wrote a
thesis "Thomas Campion and the Art of English

Poetry," and was made assistant professor of English literature in the National University.

MacDonagh at the time would have welcomed a reasonable settlement of Irish political conditions   Two years after its angry rejection by the National Convention he said to me that the country should have accepted the Councils Bill, with its control of education and its possibilities of checking financial relations between Ireland and Great Britain. I often had a vision of my friend in a Home Rule Parliament, working at social and legislative problems, and perhaps training himself to become a Minister of Education. He was, when the Home Rule Bill reached its last stages, happily married, and was the father of the child he has addressed in " Wishes for my Son." In the end, the Home Rule question became something different from an adjustment of legislation as between Great Britain and Ireland. Its granting or its withdrawal was made a question of military preparation and racial manliness. Then the Nationalists created their Volunteers and Thomas MacDonagh took a place on the Executive and the command of a corps.

A poet with a tendency towards abstractions, a scholar with a bent towards philology—these were the aspects Thomas MacDonagh often showed when he expressed himself in letters. But what was fundamental in him rarely went into what he wrote. That fundamental thing was an eager search for something that would have the whole devotion of his being. Eagerness, search, devotedness—these are the characters that for me spell out his most lovable spirit. He had too a powerful ambition. With his short figure, his scholar's brow and his dominating nose he looked like a man of the Gironde— a party, by the way, that he often spoke of.

In the old heroic story Finn is asked what music he preferred. He spoke of the song of the blackbird, the scream of the eagle, the sound of the waterfall, the bay of the hounds. And when Oisin was asked what music delighted him he said " The music of the thing that happens." Thomas MacDonagh could have made the lofty answer of Oisin. He surely loved the music of the thing that happened. He followed the music that meant the language revival, the music that meant the Volunteer movement, the music that meant insurrection. And at last he stood up to the music that meant defeat and death. In memory of him we will often repeat the words he has written in this book. " It is well for us that our workers are poets and our poets workers. . . . And it is well too that here still that cause which is identified, without underthought of commerce with the cause of God and Right and Freedom, the cause which has been the great theme of our poetry, may any day call the poets to give their lives in the old service."

PADRAIC COLUM.

LITERATURE IN IRELAND

——◄•●•►——

I.

INTRODUCTORY AND GENERAL.

IN literature it will be found that the characteristic
contribution of each great master is two-fold. The
new message comes in a new form, the new wine in
a new vessel. No great poet has really put new wine
into old bottles. To English Chaucer gave a fresh
literature and a fresh mode of literary expression. One
part of his gift was a narrative poetry never since surpassed.
The vessel in which he presented a quantity of it, the
couplet to which later was given that high title of heroic,
was perhaps more rare and new than his other forms.
So Dryden, with the first fine vintage of literary criticism, gave that modern prose of the living voice, made
good at last for all the purposes of prose. So Milton,
to take an example that may be at once accepted, that
need not be explained and proved, with his epic poetry

gave that epic blank verse of such different poise from the already perfect dramatic. So Pope, with the poetry of the intellect (to damn it with a paradox) gave the heroic couplet, wrought to a second perfection—perhaps for that alone a second-rate master. One need not drag in Shakespeare, from whose work you can prove anything ; and one need not make a list of the masters of English or other literatures. A new verse, a new style in prose— something that can be weighed and measured—a new manifestation that can be seen, comes always with that new imponderable, incommensurable, elusive something which one knows to be fine literature, but which cannot be tested by any such sure standards. I will say that poetry may be not only a criticism of life, as Matthew Arnold thought, but an interpretation of life, or, at its highest, an illumination of life. The ancient Irish critic of the *Triads* had this for one of his marks of the poet, *imbas forosna*, knowledge that illumines. I will say this. I know well enough what I mean by these terms. But when I come to apply them to some actual piece of literature, more especially of new literature, they help me little. This new thing is unlike all the fine literature that I know. Is it a criticism of life ? Is it an interpretation ? Is it an illumination ? What really is life ? When so illuminated does it change and become different from all that we know by experience ?

What right have we to limit it to experience ? Are we looking only for the experience of the intellectual thing, forgetting the intuitive ? Are not these terms of criticism only words of praise and no standards at all ? And so—though with the old standard of beauty we have set aside the old standard of truth—so back to the tragic query, What is truth ?

If, in the course of these studies, I have said that poetry is a criticism, or an interpretation, or an illumination of life, I use the terms with reference to work that has fallen back into perspective—not work in the near shadow of which we stand. To answer one of my questions just put, I use them as terms of praise, not as tests for the next poem that comes.

On the other hand one can really, if only in a negative way, judge the form of a new work. Forms change and become outworn though the essential stuff of literature may be the same from age to age. A five-act play, written now in just Shakespeare's verse, if such a thing could be done, would be something of a sham antique. Good Tennysonian blank verse betrays many pretentious poems. The imitators of Blake and Browning have not surpassed their masters. Whitman, however, the most confident of us cannot condemn so easily. He may be but another eccentric. He may be the great innovator. The futurists may be charlatans, or fools, or lunatics.

They may be prophets. The difference of their manner from the good old ways does not prove their rightness or their greatness ; but the hostile critics of their works use words and weapons so like those used against other work that survived attack and afterwards became right and great and good, that one cannot lightly join them. Most writers who made daring departures in form merely wandered off and were lost. Yet the new path of some pioneer to-day may prove the right turning for all. The path of glory in literature has not been, as many appear to think, the broad and easy way. It is now beaten broad enough—up to a certain point, reached a generation ago—by the feet of many who have followed in the tracks of men who discovered things in the heavens and on earth, not keeping their eyes on their feet, and of men who ran hither and thither after splendid adventures, and of men who fared far to the east and to the west lured by the voices of strange peoples. It is not the obvious straight path that leads from height to height.

As with the masters, so with what we have still to call the movements The Renaissance, in whose mode we are still, or have been till now, had its new wine and its new vessels. The so-called classic and romantic movements within it have theirs, each stage of each remembered by the double gift of a master. The gift to literature of the writers whom I count as of the Irish Mode—

putting this term of mine in the place of that vague and illogical Celtic Note—is likewise double. For the reasons which I here set forth, I criticise as much the form of the work as the import, though to me, of course, that import is its chief worth. I make experimental studies to satisfy myself that this is at least a mode, distinctive and apart.

The Renaissance, with the discoveries of Copernicus and Galileo, the discoveries of Columbus and his followers ; later such things as the discovery of the law of gravitation, the Cartesian philosophy, the French Revolution, Darwin's theory of evolution : these have profoundly affected European literature. They have not similarly affected literature in Ireland This is not to say of course that in Ireland writers are still likely to write of the earth as the centre of the solar system, of epicycles and the rest. It is to say that literature here has not had just that education which is common to the other literatures of western Europe. Those literatures have been, as I have said, up to these days, parts of the Renaissance. In them the authority of the ancients has held :

" And Boileau still in right of Horace sways."

That word " authority " holds a world of meaning in this matter. Another word of great content is

" intellectual." Intellectualism is the Renaissance. When in the place of that clear standard we set those pillars of cloud and of fire known to the spiritual intuitions, the day of the Renaissance is done ; the forms of Renaissance literature decay.

In Ireland some literature has kept the old way familiar to the Middle Age.

Let me not anticipate my conclusion. Let me make clear my meaning of things I have said above.

In his sonnet, *On first looking into Chapman's Homer*, Keats has set together the three great influences of Elizabethan literature : the classic world, its art, its literature, its story, represented by Homer ; the new astronomy that raised adventure to the skies ; the new discoveries that opened to the view new seas and lands beyond the peaks of Darien. Keats himself, who might have lived long enough for me a child to know him, owned the same influences. He touched in not too late a day the beautiful mythology of Greece ; yet he felt other influences too. *La Belle Dame sans Merci*, though he may have disdained it, shows that another wind blew on him at hours. So too with the other arts in his time. They derived from Italy, and through Italy from Greece. To our eyes even the Romantic era has a classic quality, a sense of repose almost, compared with the disturbance now taking place in all the arts. All the forms are suffering change. It would seem that the mind (its outlook and its inlook, if one may say so) is suffering change and demanding different forms of expression. This, since the establishment of Impressionism, is more easily admitted in painting than in literature, as indeed since Wagner it may be more easily admitted in music too ; but to anyone conversant with modern literature the same change of order is evident here. Compare modern poems and modern novels, the claim of which to serious recognition cannot be denied, with similar works of the previous ages and you will at once perceive that the difference here too is due to the introduction of Impressionism and Wagnerism. To us as to the ancient Irish poets, the half-said thing is dearest. The rhythm made by an emotion informs the poem and so recreates the emotion. As to the mystic, so to the lyric poet the unknown transcends the known. The purely rational, purely intellectual way of expression does not lead from it and so to it. I am not writing here of European literature in general, or of English literature in particular. I am introducing a movement that is important to English literature, because it is in part a revolt from it—because it has gone its own way, independent of it, though using for its language English or a dialect of English. I am treating it as a separate thing ; and all that I have said so far is said rather by way of comparison, to set it in its true light.

It enters literature at a period which seems to us who are
of it as a period of disturbance, of change. Its mode
seems strange to the critics and to the prosodists of the
old order. Its mode is not that of the Futurists or the
writers of *vers libres* ; but still, coming with the work
of these, it stands as another element of disturbance, of
revolution ; it is comparatively free from the old authority imposed by the Renaissance, while the other elements
in this disturbance are rebelling against that authority ;
it is the mode of a people to whom the ideal, the spiritual,
the mystic, are the true, while theirs is that of people who
seek, however blindly, for a truth beyond the easy truth
which is the beauty of the romantics, who will not admit
that this identification of a rational truth and a rational
beauty is all they know on earth or all they need to know.
Beyond this I would not urge the parallel ; but this it is
necessary to note in order to understand the reception
given to the Irish Mode. It has come in its due time.
Mangan and Callanan in the first half of the nineteenth
century tuned the harp that is now ringing to the hands
of many. Ears that in the older days would not have
listened to the rarest music of that harp are now atten-
tive to every tone. The poets of this mode have till
now been ignorant of the parallel movement ; they have
taken little or no note of the new writers of free verse
or of the futurists. Yet their work to the coming age

may appear one with the work of these. And indeed there is a near kinship. The freedom being sought now elsewhere has long been enjoyed here. One might reasonably argue that Macpherson, so great an influence in the Romance, was the first of the free verse men—that his work marks the beginning, not merely of the Romantic Era of European literature, but of that freedom of the new time set against the old Authority of the Renaissance.* In such a train we should come to regard the Romantic Era as the dawn of Freedom, not the noon of Liberty under Law. Should we follow such a train we should not at the same time forget that, as the work of each great author may be an epitome of a whole literature, with parts representing all the stages—as, in English literature, we find in Shakespeare, in Milton, in Wordsworth, in Keats, both the classic and the romantic, both the meditative and the lyric—parts which are monuments of the central tradition, obedient to Authority, and parts which are the promise of the Freedom to be, with examples of its mode, with stones for the building of its monuments, and even the first chambers of its towers, as finely shaped and firmly built as any added in its full day ; so the eras dovetail and interlace ; so the colours shade into one another ; so always side by

---

* One finds free verse in Mangan, too,—in *Kidder*.

side go reaction and radicalism ; so the classic has not
died and romance has but revived ; and still there is
nothing new under the sun and all novelty is but oblivion.
These things we should not forget ; but these should not
at the same time hold us from the perception of change :
they are limitations of the law, not the law itself. The train
which I have indicated would lead us to look for a transformation of literature similar, not to the transformation
which we call the Romance (itself a beginning, a first
stirring of this greater change) but to the Renaissance,
the influence and authority of which it would end. Such
a train would give a high importance to the Irish mode.

In the Bible, English, as other West-European literatures, has had, since the Renaissance, a second great
source of tradition and authority. A third might
have been found in that so-called folk literature, the
ballads, the wonder-tales and fragments of old prose
epics that survived the change wrought in the schools.
Various strands of the other two materials were caught
by various hands and worked into the fabric of the
literature. Strands of this material were caught at
now and again—by Sir Philip Sidney, by Addison,—
but missed and merely looked at, not held and woven
in. The strands hung down beside the others with
which all hands were busy. They have been used now
these hundred years. Is the new fabric made of them

so different from the old that it will tear away from it
now that new weight of the stuff wrought in these days
is added ?   For beyond that folk literature we might
trace the Gaelic influence direct, never quite absent
even under the Renaissance, now present and potent.

The work which I have set myself to do in some of these
studies is rather to examine the one aspect of literature in
Ireland than can be examined and treated in terms of
criticism.   To serve this I have dealt with the language,
the Irish dialect of English, if it can be called a dialect.
I have not with some modern writers made much ado
about chance idioms.   The absolute construction found
in Charles Wolfe's poem, *On the Burial of Sir John
Moore*:

"And we far away on the billow,"

has been traced by most writers on this subject to Gaelic
origin, and flaunted as a modern Irishism.   Of course
the phrase translates word for word into Irish : " agus
sinne i bhfad ar an bhfairrge " ; but then the idiom
occurs in English too, easily enough and early enough.
I came across an instance of it the other day in Pepy's
Diary, and to-day another in Jane Austen.   Pepy's :
" 1665, 20th July.   The bell always going.   This day
poor Robin Shaw at Blackwell's died, and Blackwell
himself in Flanders."   Jane Austen, in *Pride and
Prejudice*, Chapter VIII. : " Yes, and her petticoat—

I hope you saw her petticoat.   Six inches deep in mud,
I am absolutely certain, and the gown which had been
let down to hide it not doing its office."   More important
than such phrases is word order.   Though in Anglo-
Irish speech we keep in the main the order of English,
not of Irish, even in the most literal translations, yet
the Irish way of emphasis is kept.   The sentence, " I
came from town," may have four meanings according
to the emphasis, or rather the voice stress.   An Irishman
may use this sentence as it stands for those four meanings
too ; but in general he introduces the verb which corresponds to the Irish verb of identity* and brings into the
emphatic position after it the particular word of the
four which he wishes to stress.   Thus he will use such a
sentence as " It is from town I came " instead of the
original stressed on the last syllable, and even such a
Gaelicism as " It is how I came from town," instead of
the original stressed on the second.   It will be seen that
in these substitutes the words do all the work.   The
voice does not exert itself.   This goes with the even way
of speech that ranks equal with Irish metrics and Irish
music as one of the most important factors of the Irish
mode of versification, in English.   I merely indicate these

---

* *Is.*   There are three distinct verbs in Irish corresponding
to three senses of the verb to be.   The examples in the text
will show one use of the verb of identity.

matters here, as I have dealt fully with them in the studies which follow. Another matter worth indicating is the phonetic difference between Irish and English. This, of course, has to do with that Irish way of speech which I have set down as one of the three great influences on the versification of this Mode.

So much then for the form : of the spirit, the genius, of this literature, and therefore of this people, I could not trust myself to speak : I could not trust myself to set out with certainty Irish characteristics, or to point out the probable trend of the literature. This is an age of beginnings rather than of achievements ; for a hundred years now writers in this land have been translating, adapting, experimenting—working as the writers of the sixteenth century worked in many countries. The translations which have survived are those most in consonance with the genius of the country An age of beginnings : what the next age or the ripeness of this may bring, one can only guess at.

Does some one say that I shirk work necessary in one portion of my field—that criticism can deal surely with national characteristics ? Whimsicality is an Irish characteristic as definite as any—that drollery so different from wit proper, so different from humour proper, going waywardly with an inconsequence that one knows to be natural Yet what is one to say of it ? To collect samples would be stupid work, and the result as stupid as any book of bulls. " You're cosy and easy up there, Johnny," I heard a man say at a football match in Dublin to a friend who watched from a tree. The day was windy. " Aye, begad," said Johnny, " blown about by every breeze, like a bee on a posy." In this, to be sure, I might find certain graces of diction, the half-rhyme of " cosy " and " easy," with the echo of it in " posy," and the alliteration of Johnny's b's, to say nothing of the rhythm. These things are to be found in almost all Irish speech of a humorous turn. " Come into my arms, you bundle of fun," is the more delightfully humorous for its obvious rhythm. But that examination would again be of the sound rather than of the sense, and would be to me gruesome work.

Different from such is the great informing soul of a large body of our lyric poetry, of our oratory, and of much of the rest of our literature—" the cause that never dies," the ideal held always by the Gaelic race that once dominated Europe—now held by the heir and successor of that race here, the Irish. The calamities of our history have given a voice to that cause. The constancy of our race has given pride to that voice. " It is easy," says a contemporary good critic,* " to be patriotic in the days

---

* A.C.H. of *Poetry,* a Chicago monthly.

of a country's adversity ; for then patriotism means
something very personal. Its root is personal, no doubt,
although that does not prevent the emotions transcending
the bounds of a merely selfish personal motive. But the
fact that the sentiment is emotional and personal, rather
than abstract and rhetorical, is what constitutes its living
force. When a country is in adversity, then this emotion
is continuously active. It is a passion which absorbs
all the energies. So much so that it completely enlists
the services not only of men of action and practical life,
but also of the contemplatives, the poets, the dreamers,
for whom this emotion, like others, becomes trans-
muted into something beyond the personal emotion.
. . . . It is easy for us to appreciate the Irishman's
zealous love for Ireland, the celebration of Bengal by
the great East Indian poet, or the passionate spirit of the
Roumanian folk-songs. Not only have these the direct
motive of adversity, the minor note of which has been so
much in sympathy with the spirit of the last century's
literary movement, but they are all deep-rooted in the
tradition which has had its earliest expression in folk-songs
and legends—always an enduring basis for subsequent
poets and artists, and an integral part of the blood and
bone of the people."

This writer has stated almost sufficiently for me the
case of Irish patriotism as an inspiration. It is never far

off. Many strong workers in the national movements are good poets too ; no Irish poet or dreamer knows the day when he may be called into action in the ancient fight. More than that, nearer here than elsewhere seems the day that Ruskin desired for his own country when her soldiers should be her tutors, and the captains of her army, captains also of her mind* ; for here the professional barriers do not keep life and letters apart, and the national cause survives politics. I have heard a friend of mine state on the authority of one of the new philosophers, that hunger and sex are the two wheels of progress. If so, no doubt progress here must be set down to the account of hunger. Sex counts for little enough in Irish or Anglo-Irish literature. Mr. Synge's people talk more of it than others, but even they do not give it the importance that it has in most modern literature ; they do not talk of it in the decadent, suggestive way, however morbid the analysis of their creator. They talk of it rather like the Irish peasantry, whose language is at times coarse enough while their conduct is almost impeccably proper. Such progress as as there is would in this philosophy be set down to hunger ; but that seems to me a mean way of judging life. Our ideals, national and religious, are powerful and holy.

---

* *The Crown of Wild Olive :* War.

Such a matter-of-fact politician as Parnell exhorted us to national effort, not in terms of hunger and profit, but in terms of tradition and the sacred gift of the ideal for which we have stood against tramplings and settlements these thousand years : " Keep the fires of the nation burning." This " terrible and splendid trust," this " heritage of the race of kings," this service of a nation without a flag, but " with the lure of God in her eyes," has endowed some of our poetry with meanings that must be lost to all but those baptized in our national faith. To some lyrics of Thomas Moore the heroism and death of Robert Emmet, his early friend, gave a quality of emotion far deeper than the sentiment that usually fills his verse. George Brandes, in his *Main Currents of Nineteenth Century Literature* has shown the importance of this poetry of revolt in Anglo-Irish. In Gaelic there is a symbolic poetry of patriotism that rises far higher. Lyrics like *Eamonn an Chnuic, Druimfhionn Donn Dilis* and a hundred other such are without parallel in any literature that I know of—and this too though, or perhaps because, the Gaelic poetry of the later centuries is but a wandering voice. The old courts of the kings and the halls of the chiefs were in the earlier times centres of culture—of art, of learning, of song. These gone, the profession of poet lost dignity There was no metropolitan life in Gaelic Ireland. The Gaelic language had

c

not the fixing and centralizing of the printing press, a loss or absence which, given other advantages, is an advantage in itself, here only a thing to note as counting for something. From this Gaelic source Anglo-Irish inherited a folk poetry at times of almost indescribable tenderness and beauty, but narrow in range and of little variety

As in other countries, the drama in Ireland is a foreign introduction, and an introduction of too recent date, speaking nationally, to be yet subject for criticism. It is probably certain that some of the drama of the present day in English will stand higher in literature than any of at least the last century. There has been a revival of the poetic drama. The new drama of ideas, of criticism of life, is a serious and important form of literature. Like almost all other forms, it has been influenced by, and is in part a development of, that most popular of all forms, the novel. In prose, satire is perhaps the form surest of enduring appreciation. The drama of modern Ireland, in English, is in the main poetic and satiric. It seems indeed not free from the faults of its time, or rather of the time just gone by in some of the continental countries,— not free from the faults of impressionism, of quasi-scientific Ibsenism, of unreal gloom and of shallow cynicism. It is its virtue to have shown the way back to the life of the people and back to poetry

One inspiration of literature remains to mention in this cursory introduction. That mysticism, which in all literatures is the promise and earnest of great poetry, has come here in these days. The bulk of the mystical poetry I cannot claim for Anglo-Irish on account of the limitations of form and language which I have set to these studies. It is, nevertheless, the growth of this soil, of the passivist, contemplative character of this people, so long enduring and so certain of the right—the good. Of the science of mysticism, so to call it, these Irish poets know little by study or instruction, though one is tempted to think that with two or three of them, writers of fame, mysticism is an exteriority, a garment borrowed from the grammarians of this science of the saints. It is, unfortunately, not difficult to give to vague nothings set in verse an appearance of the mystery of St. John of the Cross. But St. John, since I mention him, would not approve of this perhaps uncharitable judgment ; and indeed in no matter more than this is criticism vain.

These studies are then a first attempt to find standards for criticism in Irish and Anglo-Irish literature, more especially in Anglo-Irish poetry. The good critic must judge a work or a creature in relation to its nature, its aim or purpose, its aspiration—in terms of what it is, not of what it might have been if otherwise designed and made. It is vain to blame the angel for not showing the steady utility of the cow, and to blame the cow for lacking the light and service of the angel. But, before coming even to the right way of judgment, the critic must discover the nature of the work or creature. I try to discover the nature of some literature produced in Ireland.

———————

II.

ANGLO-IRISH LITERATURE.

WE speak of Anglo-Irish literature as we speak of Elizabethan literature, of the literature of the Restoration
age, or another, as a province of English literature, confined in the place of its production as those others in
their periods, and with that difference between place and
time, between race and succession. A better analogy
than those that I have mentioned, Elizabethan and
Restoration, would seem to be Scots literature, but I
have avoided that at the beginning in order to avoid the
confusion that constantly follows such comparison.
The writers of the Restoration period of English literature
succeeded in natural order to those of the Elizabethan.
Dryden refers to Shakespeare and Ben Jonson as "the
writers of the last age." Scots literature was born own
brother to English, the literature of men of the lowland
race ; and the blood relationship has proved a strong
bond. The literature produced in the English language
in Ireland during the nineteenth century had no such
rights of succession to previous epochs of English

literature as had the work of Dryden to the work of Ben Jonson ; it had no such claim of kinship to any as had the work of King James I. of Scotland, of William Dunbar and of Gawin Douglas to the work of Chaucer   And Scots writers have from the beginning recognised that kinship. In his lovely *Lament for the Makaris*, after having bewailed the insecurity of life :

> " No stait in Erd heir standis sicker ;
>   As with the wynd wavis the wicker,
>   So wavis this warldis vanite :—
>   *Timor Mortis conturbat me,*"

and mentioned those of all " Estatis " who go unto death :

> " He takis the campion in the stour,
>   The captain closit in the tour
>   The lady in bour full of bewte,"

Dunbar enumerates the dead poets, beginning :

> " He has done petuously devour
>   The noble Chaucer, of makaris flour,
>   The Monk of Bury and Gower, all three :
>   *Timor Mortis conturbat me,*"

and proceeding with a long list of Scots poets, some of them else unknown.   To the Scots poets Chaucer was as Dunbar says in another poem,

> " As in oure tong ane flour imperial."

Anglo-Irish literature is then different in its origins, in its history, in its tradition, from Scots. At its weakest and poorest it is a weak and poor imitation of the poor contemporary work of Englishmen. At its richest and strongest it has qualities of its own not to be found in the work of any Englishmen of the time. And it is distinctly a new literature, the first expression of the life and ways of thought of a new people, hitherto without literary expression, differing from English literature of all the periods not with the difference of age but with the difference of race and nationality. That race is the Irish race, now mostly English-speaking. That life, those ways of thought expressed in the new literature, are the life and ways of the Gael, modified by the change of language from Gaelic to English and by the things that brought about that change, but still individually Gaelic, spiritually, morally, socially (in all the ways that matter in literature), filled with memories of the old Gaelic literature, moving to the rhythm of Irish music (a thing that matters very much to the metric of the new poetry), rich in fresh metaphor, very different from the petrified boughs of imagery that do duty for green branches in many admired works of this age. The people are agricultural people, fresh from the natural home of man, the fields and the country, busy with the oldest and simplest things of life, people who have not grown up in the streets of towns among the artificialities of civilisation, with traditional memories of brick and plaster. The Anglo-Irish literature that matters has not come from the English spoken for hundreds of years in the Pale, in Dublin and its surroundings, by the English garrison in Ireland, but from the new English speakers of the country whose fathers or grandfathers spoke only Irish.

In later studies I shall have to deal on the one hand with the character and growth of the English language in Ireland and on the other hand with many aspects of the Gaelic language and literature. Here I wish simply to show, without stating an opinion as to the benefit or the pity of it, that an Anglo-Irish literature of individual value, a literature of worth in English, expressing or interpreting or criticising life in Ireland was possible only when the people whose life was the subject matter spoke the English language and spoke it well, and when Irish writers had attained what may be called the plenary use of the English language—such use as had decidedly not been attained by some of the Gaelic writers who wrote occasionally in English also—when, in a word, Irish writers and Irish readers were able to practise and to appreciate the art of English poetry and the art of English prose. When this point had been reached by new writers who were themselves of the people, the English-speaking

Irish people, then this literature appeared and not till then. The so-called Anglo-Irish literature of the eighteenth century was no such thing. Certain Irishmen, going to England, adopted English manners, expressed English or European life, referred to themselves as Englishmen. They occasionally introduced into their work what would now be called a little local colour, tinted with memories of their early Irish days ; but for the rest they were as much out of Ireland in spirit as in body. Occasionally too they introduced to their readers English-speaking Irishmen, but these were either caricatures or were obviously only half articulate in their new speech

At the same time Gaelic literature continued, but with the repression by law of Irish learning, the language fell towards the position of a patois, and its later literature is mostly of folk tales and folk poems, sometimes very beautiful, but in general poor by comparison with the monuments of previous epochs.

At the same time also some Irish writers who did not leave their own country, or at least lived mostly in Ireland, emulated their emigrant brethren and became English authors, never indeed of great importance, but frequently very ingenious, writing in English either of a life that they did not know at first hand or of a life that they could

not express in this language, and so always something
out of joint.

One small body of poems has the timber and the sap
of true literature, but wants the shaping and the
higher graces. This consists of the street ballads, almost
altogether of Dublin origin. If one can have regrets
in such a matter as literary criticism and history, if one
can wish that things had ever gone otherwise, one must
regret that Dublin did not, in the eighteenth or early
nineteenth century produce an Irish Villon, a University
wit capable of writing a poem like *The Night before Larry
was Stretched*. The capital produced none such ; and
the ballads, religious and ribald and rebelly, are frag-
mentary and spasmodic : they created no fine literary
tradition.   No author arose of the more urbane or of the
more rural forms of literature who was at once sufficiently
Gaelic to express the feeling of the central Irish tradition
and sufficiently master of English style to use it as one
uses the air one breathes. George Darley's references
to Irish history, his use of Irish clan names, are weak and
colourless. Curran's Irish phrases are ungrammatical,
Drennan, at his simplest a fine poet, in his eloquent poems
stammers twenty book-words to fill the place of one true
epithet.

I would not be taken as wishing in any way to belittle
the intentions of these writers or of those others men-

tioned above, who were, as I have said, something out
of joint. They lived according to their lights. They
did the work they found to their hands. They were not
Gaelic, or at least they were not in touch with the Gaelic
tradition. They thought they knew a better thing and
followed it. Most of them recognised as their kith only
the small English-speaking fragment of Ireland ; and that
fragment had not the culture, the enthusiasm or the
intensity of life that breaks into poetry or eloquence. Some
of the early Anglo-Irish writers, not the emigrants like
Goldsmith, Swift and Sheridan, anticipated the cohesion
of the English-speaking Irish race, and began to translate,
adapt and imitate Gaelic literature.   Irish music was one
of the most powerful influences in the work of Thomas
Moore. Others adopted the sentiments of the only
articulate popular politics of their day, the politics of
Grattan and the sympathetic Protestant patriots, the
patriotism of the Pale, a very different thing from the
national feeling of the real Irish people ; but these, such
of them as Charles Macklin, on his return to Ireland,
appealed still only to Dublin audiences. The day of
Anglo-Irish literature had not arrived, because the Anglo-
Irish author could not yet be the poet of his little clan.
The old inspirations that had moved poets in this land
were not breathed into the souls of those men of alien
speech.

I have so far used without definition the term Anglo-
Irish. Like many terms of the kind, it is misleading and
awkward, yet so well established by usage that it can
scarcely be dispensed with. It can be applied only to
language, and so to literature. There is, of course, no
Anglo-Irish race, though many Irishmen have English
blood in their veins. The invaders who came at the end
of the twelfth century, under Strongbow and his fellows,
were Flemings and Welsh, not English. The English who
were planted in Ireland under Mary, Elizabeth, James,
Cromwell, and their successors, formed a small portion of
the people, and though they brought the language which
is now spoken by the majority of the Gaelic people, they
made little enough impress on the race that they dis-
possessed and drove westwards. With the language, the
Anglo-Irish dialect, English as we speak it in Ireland, to
use Dr. Joyce's phrase, I shall deal in a later study
Here it is well at once to make clear that the term Anglo-
Irish literature is applied very rarely to the meagre writings of the planters ; it is worth having as a term only to
apply to the literature produced by the English-speaking
Irish, and by these in general only when writing in
Ireland and for the Irish people. We shall find some few
writers such as Lionel Johnson and Nora Chesson of the
last generation who, born and living altogether out of
Ireland, were yet so much in love with Ireland, in sym-

pathy with the Irish Mode, in consonance with the Irish rhythm of life and literature, in converse with Irish people and out of converse with others, that they must be counted of the number who come within the narrowest definition of our term. So also one or two of the best Gaelic writers of our time have no personal knowledge of this country. On the other hand some of us who live in Ireland, of Gaelic stock, even of Gaelic speech, are for all that more Greek than Gael. It is difficult to fix the zone ; but by the time we have analysed some characteristics of Irish literature in the two languages and verified the qualities of the Irish Mode, though we shall probably have shortened the list of Anglo-Irish authors, it is to be hoped that by doing so we shall have enhanced its value. For the rest, Ireland can now afford to contribute of her new wealth to the common literature of the English language, keeping this characteristic literature of her own apart.

Before proceeding to this analysis and verification it is well to examine origins, tradition, history and other influences, beginning with the question of language and literature.

III.

LANGUAGE AND LITERATURE.

" OUR morning star," wrote old Archbishop Trench, " Chaucer yet ushered in no dawn which was on the point of breaking." The well of English undefiled was indeed for just two hundred years alone the one rich source of English literature. Then many waters broke from the ground of the English language and the stream flowed strong.

The date of the beginning of the *Canterbury Tales*, 1386, is a useful one to count by. English, for quarter of a century the language of the Courts of Law, had then just replaced French as the language taught in the schools. Chaucer's important contemporary, Gower, was on the point of turning from the French and Latin of his previous works to the English of his third poem, *Confessio Amantis*. The promise of an English literature must have appeared fair   Yet the language had to wait long for its fulfilment. It had to go to school again, and to a different school ; it had to unlearn and to learn. It had to mellow its voice in silence ; it had to train its members in patience, before it could attain the utterance and the gesture of its new youth and its prime. The language of Chaucer had not in his day become the national language. His contemporary, Langland, used a different syntax. The Anglo-Norman people, of which Chaucer was a good type, had to mingle and to weld before its thought and emotion could find expression in the modern English of the last three hundred and fifty years. The literature of a dialect is tuneful only to the accompaniment of a central literature.

It is significant that no English poet of importance has followed in Chaucer's way. He is the best, indeed the only, true narrative poet of the language. He is in a certain sense the least lyric of the great English poets. In this one quality of his work he is so much akin to French poets that one is tempted to set it up with other barriers and divide him from English literature proper.

I urge this matter here with instance because I wish to make clear the connection in Ireland between language and literature, to show that though in the seventeenth and eighteenth centuries an Irish Chaucer might have arisen, turning from the Gaelic of his clan to the English of the Pale, he would have been only a morning star too, not the rising sun. Of course there are differences in the conditions and the rest, but the main consideration is that a literature with the seeds of succession in it comes in the

mother language of the teller and of the listener, of the
singer and of those who take up the refrain.   The simple
fact is that, as, according to a certain Scot, there must
always be two parties to a joke, the man who makes it
and the man who sees it ; so, surely, there must be two
parties to the making of a literature ; and the second
party must be capable of full appreciation.   The poet is,
no doubt, as I have said elsewhere in this volume, his own
first audience   His poetry is a matter between himself and
himself.   If others afterwards come and share his joy, the
gain is theirs   But he is sensitive to the emotions and sympathies of his country and time   He is, whether he like
it or not, the heir of the ages, in possession of the passing
period and of the future.   He himself is the poet and
himself the auditor ; but his second self is a critic, and to
be a critic is to know other men and to appreciate the
tastes of other men, and these others almost of necessity
his countrymen.   He is most blessed when his countrymen are fresh for literature—which is not to say that
a writer, whatever his genius, could initiate a separate
literature merely by seeking and finding a people, even
his own people, without a modern literature.   His doing
so depends on the people, on the state of their culture,
and more particularly on the state of their ideals, national,
religious, mystical.   And when he finds them with all
these qualities, he must speak not merely of his people,

but to them and for them, discovering them to themselves, expressing them for themselves. William Carleton made the mistake, during one part of his career at least, of writing about Ireland for a foreign audience. He hoped, as he says in a letter from London to his daughter, to reach a popularity equal to that of Dickens or Thackeray, " and consequently to have the English publishers at my feet and willing to come to my own terms." Carleton knew Irish, and might possibly, some think, have been the Gaelic Mistral—if he had been a patriot. As it was he fell between two stools. The Irish people proper were deaf to his word : the English people listened while moved by the horrors of the Famine of 1847, and then turned a deaf ear too A Molière that cannot interest his washerwoman will not interest the passers by.

English literature has had some difficulty in getting rid of the phraseology, the inversions, the poetic words, the cumbrous epithets, the mannerisms, of its pastoral and of its genteel days. It has, indeed, not yet got quite rid of them. The English reading of the early Anglo-Irish writers filled their memories with those old, stale things ; but the individual Anglo-Irish literature of which I write has no such lumber It is the record of the speech of the people, the living word—sometimes, no doubt, heightened, to use the old phrase, but of a directness that Wordsworth would have adored. Indeed it

D

would seem that the desire of Wordsworth for a literature written only in the common language of the people is best fulfilled in the work produced in Ireland.   His own work rarely attains the level balance of such poems as *Michael:* the weak prose of some of his peasant verse errs as much on one side as does the heightened diction of such a poem as *The Affliction of Margaret* on the other.   Of course the very latest of the Anglo-Irish writers have had something of Wordsworth's difficulty.   Mr. W. B. Yeats, who, for all the unearthliness of much of his work, has used in his lyrics the most direct colloquial phrase, confesses this in some of his poems.   And in a letter to the writer he has said :   " I remember as an important event getting rid of the word ' rife.' "   In passing, one may remark that this striving after colloquial directness has its dangers too The latest poems of Mr. Yeats show that he has failed to recognise an important fact of English grammar, the function of the conventional word order.   Admit that poetic licences should be no more allowed than other licences, but examine poetry's charter of liberty before you tear it up.   It is an older charter than that of prose.

One of the distinctions of this Anglo-Irish literature that marks it off from the mere epochs of English literature proper is its independence of obsolete species.   It matters nothing to Irish writers of the day that English has had

in due succession its lyric, its dramatic, its epic, its
didactic poetry and then the new lyric of romanticism,
inspired by the Celtic breath ;* that the Elizabethan
prose writers, even Bacon, set no standard, made no
lasting moulds, were again morning stars and not day
stars ; that prose went on many anvils before it was
fit for all its uses ; that it has to-day become at once
keen and flexible only after that long tempering. In
spite of the self-consciousness of the age, in spite of the
world influences felt here, in spite of all our criticism,
the Irish poets and writers (those that are truly Anglo-
Irish) are beginning it all over again in the alien tongue
that they know now as a mother tongue   They delight
not in the ink-horn terms of the English literary succession, but in the rich living language of a people
little affected by book-lore, a people standing but a little
way on the English side of the crossways, remembering
something of the syntax or the metaphor of Gaelic,
much of the rhythm, inventing mostly for itself its metaphor from the things of its life, things known at first
hand.

Once more this is not to say that the literature can grow
and progress now as if nothing had ever happened in the
world before—as if, for instance, the Renaissance had never

---

* I am here claiming the influence rather of Macpherson
than of Blake and others.

been and as if the Romantic Revival had not changed the
literatures of Europe. On the contrary, the things that
have happened, especially indeed the things that have
affected English literature, must powerfully affect our
literature. Indeed it has its beginnings partly in the
Romantic Revival. To find a literature that had none of
its timbers out of a previous edifice one would have to go
back to that raised in lamentation by Adam and Eve on the
loss of Paradise or of their son. This Anglo-Irish literature
knows the poetry of Romance. It gains thereby. It con-
tinues it, and has a chance of continuing in a higher mood,
given new freshness of ideas, freshness of race, independence of book tradition, and the advantage of experience shared in common with other English literature.
It departs from Romance, and still has had the advantage
of using it. But with all this, and by all this, it is a new
beginning. Some of its writers, *docti sermones utriusque
linguae*, cannot, it would seem, fail to be under current
influences. Does this detract from its claim to newness
or make it but the going on of an older literature, whether
Gaelic or English? Chaucer's work, to cite it again,
must have seemed a going on in his day—part of it a
continuation in English of the work of French poets,
and part a continuation of the work of the writers of the
old chivalrous romances and the like—with a new power
and a new note. To some who could best appreciate

the work of Langland* he must have appeared a man who " writ no language," as Spenser, in a different light, appeared to Ben Jonson.

Chaucer stands in England at the end of the Middle Ages. Between him and Spenser intervene the barbarous Wars of the Roses, Amurath succeeding Amurath, for all that Shakespeare said. The gay time of the Canterbury Pilgrims was gone, when, in the words of one of Chaucer's editors, those classes whose training fitted and disposed them to take an interest in books were in a state of gaiety at once the sequel of protracted military glory and the foster mother of artistic productivity ; when songs and pretty things were prized supremely ; when luxury was new and not quite understood ; when people wore their glories upside down ; when the ceremonial of Chivalry still retained the ostentation of devoutness and self-sacrifice. The succeeding time, so barren in literature, was, for all its ugliness, really literature in the making. The last English epic is the group of Histories in which Shakespeare dramatised the century 1385-1485.

In Ireland a period intervened between the last days of the Gaelic literature that mattered and the beginning of the new literature in the English tongue, between the hope and admiration that captured the imagination of the

---

* I have not forgotten that in the matter of vocabulary Langland is almost as much under French influence as Chaucer.

people in the days of Hugh O'Neill and Hugh O'Donnell, then of Eoghan Ruadh O'Neill, then of the Jacobites, and the new hope and anticipation that dawned in the last century and is widened to morning in this. The old Gaelic polity and culture having lost their force and their integrity, Gaelic literature became decadent in the time of the Penal Laws. Whatever the fate of the Gaelic language and literature now may be—whether its long sickness end now in death without issue, or, as some of us confidently hope, in revival and vigorous life, with renewal of the same personality, a second youth, or in the birth of a new language to utter a new literature, destined to take after its Gaelic mother only in some parts, and for the rest to bear the name of bastard in its childhood and of true-born heir in its age, a well of Irish undefiled—whatever is to be in the unknown future, it would be folly to deny the sickness, the decadence, of the immediate past. And while Irish was decadent, English was not yet able either to carry on the tradition or to syllable anew for itself here. The English-speaking population in Ireland had none of the qualities—social cohesion and integrity, culture, enthusiasm, joy, high and brave emotion—to stammer and then to utter clearly the new word. That word came to the call of the country. It came in the new language and was heard in the new day. The Renaissance that stirred England to its greatest literature brought the mingling of the cosmopolitan with the national. Here the waters have been stirred by the breath of freedom : the alien language has stirred to expression on the lips of the native people.

The revival of nationalism among the Irish subject majority following the days of the Irish Volunteers, the United Irishmen, the independent Parliament ; this nationalism, strengthened by O'Connell with Catholic Emancipation and the franchise ; this nationalism, hardened by the austere independence of Parnell, by the land war and its victorious close ; this, brought to full manhood by the renewed struggle for legislative freedom and the certainty of triumph and responsibility ; this, free from alien hope and fear, craving no ease, hearing always the supreme song of victory on the dying lips of martyrs ; this produced the unrest, the impetuous, intrepid adventure that shouts the song of joy for the sad things and for the glad things of life. The song in the new language demanded an intellectual effort that gave it a worth apart. English had to be broken and re-made to serve that song. The language that had been brought to perfection for English use, and then worn by that use, that had had the fixing of the printing press and had set the printer's word above the spoken, that language, in order to serve the different purpose of the new people, had to go back to the forge of the living speech. King

Alfred, in the first days of English prose, wrote long, awkward strings of words for sentences, with little syntactical order. The modern English author writes well-balanced, well-ordered sentences. But the Saxon King expressed more truly his thought ; in him the word order imaged more truly the thought order. The modern writer uses counters where he used coin. The modern writer cannot distinguish between his idea and the set phrase that does duty for its expression, though its terms have other meanings. He alludes to things. His prose is a hint, perfectly understood no doubt by others who know the code, but not for all that a true language. Almost perfectly it does duty for a true language to the people with whom it has grown ; better than perfectly in its poetry, which gains in suggestiveness more than its loss in concreteness. Compare the prose of this language with the superior prose of French. Compare its poetry with the far inferior poetry of French. It was, in a word, the English language, good for the English people, redolent of English history, even of the vagaries and absurdities of the history of the English people, with practical jokes and puns and stupid grammatical blunders smelling sweet with the aroma of some splendid verse—with golden lads and girls that come to dust, as chimney sweepers, and with deeds of derring-do. This language, now a courser of ethereal race now a hack between the shafts of commercialism, serving Shakespeare and the stenographer, used efficiently in William Blake's lyrics and in telegrams ; this differed in many of the ways of linguistic difference from the language of the Gael. In it the ideas of the Gael did not find easy expression.

But I have been led on a little too far. The language that was brought face to face with Irish in the eighteenth and nineteenth centuries was not the language of English commerce. The Gaelic people had for English tutors the descendants of the old English settlers, in whose mouths the language was still the language of Shakespeare. The transplanted slip of a language does not develop as does the parent tree. By comparison it rather ceases to develop. The descendants of the earliest English colonists here were found, by a new Englishman of Elizabeth's time, using " the dregs of the old ancient Chaucer English." So in our day we find in the mouths of the people what such a progressive might call the dregs of the old ancient Shakespeare English. And this was the English that had to be knit into a different com- plication from the modern complication of the central English language. For the rest, it is not only in Ireland that the phenomenon has occurred : analogous is the use of English by the American booster and by the mystic who has to express in terms of sense and wit the things of God that are made known to him in no language.

IV

IRISH AND ENGLISH.

I MENTIONED in the last chapter the possibility of the birth of a new language in this country, sprung from Irish and English. It is of course possible, but so unlikely as not to deserve further discussion. In Old English sentence structure was rudimentary. Long before the Norman Conquest the Germanic word-order at the first touch of French influence ceased to rule alone, yielding half its sway to the French. Here was a language ready for transformation. In Ireland at the present day things are very different. The syntax of the Gaelic language—and it is the syntax that matters rather than the introduction of foreign words—is fixed and in all important features not likely to undergo modification. The verb will precede its subject, the adjective will follow its noun to the end. Similarly English in Ireland will not conform to Gaelic rules. The sentence *Is the book there ?* cannot be reconciled with *Ta an leabhar ann ;* though the Irish sentence is a word for word translation of the English it means *The book is there*. But, while this is so and shall remain so, the effect of the thinking that expresses itself in the Gaelic modes has already affected and must continue to affect expression in English. *Is it the book that is there?* translates directly an Irish sentence of the same meaning. (In Irish the first word will be the verb of identity.) More important are the use in Irish of the concrete as against the English use of the abstract ; the use of the adjective in preference to the verb ; the use of peri- phrasis to avoid trusting to voice emphasis the meaning of the sentence ; the more elaborate system of verbal forms and the use of a periphrastic perfect, pluperfect and future perfect ; idioms connected with the use of prepositions ; the use of the absolute case in clauses intro- duced by *and* ; the use of the one Irish word *féin* for *even* and *self* ; the use of *do bheith ag* for *have*.

It would be tedious to give many examples of these differences. Passages quoted in subsequent chapters may be examined in this connection. Here a few will suffice. The English sentence, *That startled me*, trans- lates into Irish : *That took a start out of me. I go to Cork*, translates according to the word stressed, *It is I that am going to Cork, It is going to Cork that I am, It is to Cork that I am going.* English, *I work here*, trans- lates *I am (now) working here, I do be working here,*

I (usually) work here ; I have, had, or shall have worked
(for so long) translate *I am, was, or shall be, after working.*

Irish has undergone no very violent change in any of
its stages. Modern Irish is much more in line with
Old Irish than is Modern English with Old English. This
has saved Irish from the introduction of words that are
rather labels than names, or, to use my former image,
rather counters than coin of intrinsic worth. The name
of a thing in Irish, to take the first and most obvious of
all examples, is *ainm.* This word is used also in the
sense of the English word *noun.* Of course grammarians know of the relationship of *ainm* with *name* and
noun and *nomen* and *onoma ;* but the people to whom
such things matter more do not know A child in an
English-speaking school is taught—or used to be taught—
that the name of the thing he knows as a hand must be
parsed as a noun, and that a noun is the name of a person,
place, thing, or idea. The Irish child, learning grammar in
Irish, is told that the word *lamh* (hand) is a name (*ainm*),
that the words *leabhar, mian, fuacht, Baile Atha Cliath,
Eoin* (book, desire, cold, Dublin, John) are names.
He deals directly with his trader : there are no middle-
men with terms like *parse, noun* and the rest to make
him pay double.

On the other hand Irish has on the whole remained
unaffected by things that have very greatly affected almost

all other modern languages—by the printing press, by modern commerce, by modern science and the rest. The result is that it has not been unified. It is still rich in dialects and in variant forms. No single literary, commercial or journalistic language exists ; and, to use an Anglo-Irish phrase, there is no call for one. The vocabulary of the language is very large. It would seem that the people, thrown back on themselves and on nature, not forced to invent technical terms for the new things of civilization, have gone on with the minute study of the old things. They have named all the facets and distinguished all the moods. With this they have retained an ease for full expression that English does not know. Translation from English into Irish has more resemblance to rendering into Latin than into a modern language, like French, in spite of all the characteristic qualities of English Take this passage of De Quincey :

" It adds much to these considerations that Southern Asia is and has been for thousands of years the part of the earth most swarming with human life, the great *officina gentium.* Man is a weed in those regions."

This is Beaudelaire's French version, almost a word for word translation :

" *Ce qui ajoute beaucoup à de tels sentiments, c'est que l'Asie méridionale est, et a été, depuis des milliers d'années, la partie de la terre la plus four-*

millante de la vie humaine, la grande officina gentïum
L'homme, dans ces contrées, pousse comme l'herbe."

Latin dispenses with the redundancies, the over-
sayings, compressing a phrase into a verb :

" *Quod vero multo magis sentimus quia ex omnibus
orbis terrae gentibus Asia meridionalis per multa milia
annorum hominibus maxime redundat et semper re-
dundavit ; officina gentium, ut ita dicam, facta."*

When one comes to translate this into Irish one has
to choose between a colloquial version, easily compre-
hensible to a people which has none but a literature of
folk poems and tales, and an elaborate, emphatic version,
more carefully balanced than the Latin, with ringing
rhythms and assonances. To kill two birds with the one
stone I shall give instead of the popular Irish version
an Anglo-Irish rendering of it.

" There is that much sure. Along with that there are
far more people in South Asia than in any other land of
its size in the world, and that is how it has been for thousands of years now. A forge, or workshop of nations it
is,—*officina gentium*, as you would say—or, to say it
in another way, men grow there like weeds."

To find a literary man with a style to set against De
Quincey's one has to go back to Geoffrey Keating, the last
classic prose writer. A friend of mine has rendered the
passage into the Irish of Keating :

" *Agus ni beag d'adhbhar iongantais dúinn a mheas gurab i an Aissia theas tír is lia lánáitreabh agus is lusmhaire léirthionól agus is truime trombhuidhean do chríochaibh domhain ó chéin mhóir gus aniu, agus ni h-éigcneasta ghoirid ughdair dh'airithe* officina gentium. *mar atá, ceardcha ioltuath, di. Gá dtám ris acht ni fairsinge fás fiadhlosa i bhfearán fódbhog ioná urfhás na h-Ádhamhchloinne ar ithir na h Innia.*"

(And not little reason of wonder to us its consideration that it is South Asia that is greatest of full households and that is most plentiful of gatherings-up and that is heaviest of heavy companies of the territories of the earth from a long time ago till to-day ; and not unbecomingly certain authors call it *officina gentium,* that is, a forge of many races. Where are we then, but that not more generous the growth of wild plants in a soft sodded grassy place than the fresh growth of the Adam-clan on the arable soil of India ?)

One fears to draw conclusions too general from particular points of difference between Irish and English, in vocabulary and in grammar The one thing worth knowing in the matter, as far as we are concerned here, is that there are wide differences, which prove different mental habits, different social conditions, different literary traditions. English writing is full of metaphor that cannot be understood without knowledge of historic

events which have not affected Ireland : Shakespeare's
plays are indeed, as has been said, nothing but strings of
popular sayings.   Irish has a different set of historic
memories and of popular sayings.   These have come into
Anglo-Irish, but not in full force, and Anglo-Irish is the
simpler for it.   New images have to be supplied from
current life in Ireland ; the dialect at its best is more
vigorous, fresh and simple than either of the two languages
between which it stands.   It is indeed by its colloquial
directness that you will know the true Anglo-Irish work.
Some of our best poems indeed have no word or phrase
which alone could be labelled Irish.   On the other hand
there appear at present quantities of so-called Celtic
poems, plays, stories, which, for all their Irish phrases,
and indeed because of them, are obvious shams. A writer
of these could turn almost any sentence into his " Celtic."
Where I have said " Which are obvious shams " just now,
he would say something like this : " And, Johnny, I give
you my hand on it this night, 'tis out and out humbugs
they are surely."   One of the most powerful writers of
recent years, the late J M. Synge, was very often merely
" Celtic " in his phraseology, though far more often rich
and right.   His fault in the matter was that he crammed
his language too full of rich phrases.   He said that
he used no form of words that he had not actually
heard.   But this probably means that he took note only

of the striking things, neglecting the common stuff of speech.

In another matter Synge compares very favourably with his Irish contemporaries, his respect for the Gaelic language. He treats Irish as he would treat French or another language. Not so many of the best known Anglo-Irish writers, who treat Irish words as W. S Gilbert and such writers for comic purposes used to treat French. As *monsieur* became *mounseer* or *mosha*, the Irish *Eire* is rhymed with *fire, mo bhuachailín* becomes *ma boucheléen, slán* and *sláinte* become *shlan* and *shlainte*, against all the principles of Irish phonetics. It would be tedious and not edifying to deal thoroughly with this matter Irish has been regarded as fair game for almost any treatment. A language with an elaborate grammatical system, with delicate phonetic changes to indicate changes of sense, is treated as if it had no system and as if it could suffer nothing from barbarous mispronunciation. If the ignorance or carelessness of the writers who use it so mattered only to the Irish language, the Irish language could well afford to let it pass : it would affect it no more than does the fact that now, half a century after the time of O'Donovan and O'Curry, the Royal Irish Academy has for its president a man so grossly ignorant of the language that he is incapable of pronouncing the names of the books in its library. But to the new

E

generation of Irish readers who know the two languages,
many otherwise fine books are spoiled or at least made a
little foolish and ridiculous by the grotesque disguises
under which Irish words appear in them. And this ignorance of the authors is like that of the old sham philologists. A modern writer who made an image from the
derivation *lucus a non lucendo*, who referred to a wood
as "that which the Roman named from darkness," would
be doomed to unintelligible obscurity or to absurdity.
What then of Mr. W. B. Yeats who confesses that when
he wrote the greater number of his poems, he had hardly
considered seriously the question of the pronunciation
of Irish words, who copied at times somebody's perhaps
fanciful spelling, and at times the ancient spelling as he
found it in some literal translation, pronouncing the
words always as they were spelt ? That is, pronouncing
the words as if they were English. Mr. Yeats, however,
is quite honest in the matter. He would not, he says,
have defended his system at any time If ever he learns
the old pronunciation of the proper names he has used he
will revise the poems. He is content to affirm that he has
not treated his Irish names as badly as the mediæval writers
of the stories of King Arthur treated their Welsh names.
But Mr. Yeats is not living in the Middle Ages. Whether
we regret it or not, we cannot ignore the knowledge of
those to whom we communicate our works.   In the lines :

" The host is riding from Knocknarea
And over the grave of Clooth-na-Bare,"

nothing is gained, surely, by that extraordinary perversion
of the Irish name of the Old Woman of Beare, *Cailleach
na Béara*. The word *clooth* is not Irish ; it has no
meaning. Even for others than Irish scholars the right
word would have served as well. And—if it be not too
Philistine a question—would not :

" And over the grave of the Hag of Beare,"

have been better in this poem in English ? In his revision
of *The Wind Among the Reeds*, Mr. Yeats has changed
Irish words into English, " colleens " into " women."
Lately he has set his face against all this use of Irish
words and Irish stories ; but he cannot undo his work.
Let me admit, before passing from him, that his constant
use of the form used before him by Ferguson, has fixed
a new word in the English language. *Danaan* is impossible
in Irish, which has *Dannan* (in *Tuatha De Dannan*)
accented on the first syllable. Mr. Yeats has, as he
claims, the excuse that the words he uses are of the old
language. Mr. James Stephens has no such excuse
when he translates Miss Murphy into *Ingin Ni Murachu*,
sinning against Irish three times in three words.

No modern writer treats Greek or Latin or French or
German so. Irish goes down with the oriental languages,

Owen Roe O'Neill with Morari Row, Usheen with Alladin.   The pity of it is that it is in Ireland that Irish meets this fate.

One influence of Irish remains to be noted, perhaps the most important of all with regard to poetry, the effect of Irish rhythm, itself influenced by Irish music, on the rhythms of Anglo-Irish poetry.

English rhythm is governed by stress. In England the tendency is to hammer the stressed syllables and to slur the unstressed syllables. In Ireland we keep by comparison a uniform stress. A child in Cork, reading the word *unintelligibility*, pronounces all the eight syllables distinctly without special stress on any, though his voice rises and falls in a kind of tune or croon, going high upon the final syllable. Early Irish verse is syllabic. The lines are measured by the number of syllables. In modern verse, both Irish and English, the lines are measured by the feet, and commonly the feet differ from one another in number of syllables : each foot has one stressed syllable. In common English verse the voice goes from stress to stress, hammering the stress. In most Anglo-Irish verse the stresses are not so strongly marked ; the unstressed syllables are more fully pronounced ; the whole effect is different.

Before proceeding to examples, it is well to draw attention to the fact that some other influence, probably

French, has produced a similar effect on the verse of one or two English writers. Thus the poem of Ernest Dowson's, *Non Sum Qualis Eram Bonae sub Regno Cynarae*, which can owe, I think, nothing to Irish, has that level fall of syllables, found occasionally, as I have shown elsewhere, in the poems of Campion and one or two other of the Elizabethan's, but not again till the rise of Anglo-Irish poetry :

" I have forgot much, Cynara, gone with the wind,
Flung roses, roses, riotously with the throng,
Dancing, to put thy pale lost lilies out of mind,
But I was desolate and sick of an old passion—
    Yea, all the time, because the dance was long.
I have been faithful to thee, Cynara, in my fashion."

The earliest Anglo-Irish poems that exhibit this note we can compare with their Irish originals or with Irish poems that sing to the same air—for they are almost always songs. I quote two good examples, Callanan's *Outlaw of Loch Lene* (Killarney) and Ferguson's *Cashel of Munster*, giving the first stanza in each case. Callanan's poem can be read easily by the most formal :

" Oh, many a day have I made good ale in the glen,
    That came not of stream or malt—like the brewing of
      men.
My bed was the ground ; my roof, the greenwood above,
And the wealth that I sought one far kind glance from
    my love."

Ferguson's music is subtler :

" I'd wed you without herds, without money, or rich
    array,
And I'd wed you on a dewy morning at day-dawn grey ;
My bitter woe it is, love, that we are not far away
In Cashel town, though the bare deal board were our
    marriage bed this day ! "

One sees where Moore learned the rhythm of *The
Irish Peasant to his Mistress :*

" Through grief and through danger thy smile hath
    cheered my way,
Till hope seemed to bud from each thorn that round
    me lay ;
The darker our fortune, the brighter our pure love
    burned,
Till shame into glory, till fear into zeal was turned.
Oh ! slave as I was, in thy arms my spirit felt free,
And blessed e'en the sorrows that made me more dear
    to thee."

Sometimes we find the Gaelic internal rimes—or rather
internal rimes in the Anglo-Irish poems where in Irish
we should have assonances :

" If sadly thinking, with spirits sinking,
    Could, more than drinking, my cares compose,
A cure for sorrow from sighs I'd borrow,
    And hope to-morrow would end my woes."

One easily notes the difference between poems of this

kind with frequently recurring emphasis, marked by the rime, and poems like those of Callanan, Ferguson and Moore just quoted. In those there is that grace of the wandering, lingering, musical voice which I have noted in connection with my remark above or *unintelligibility*. Music is definitely rhythmic, with stress recurrent at regular intervals ; but as I have said elsewhere, in certain Irish tunes, set to Irish words, the music goes out of its way, as it were, to follow the varying expression of the words, which in an Irish song are all important. Mr. Carl Hardbeck of Belfast has shown this in his lectures. The tunes played by him in the ordinary way, without the words, are inferior in beauty to the tunes sung wandering with the wavering words of the old poems. Modern airs, on the contrary, tend rather to drag the words out of their way of sense. Compare the Elizabethan setting of Shakespeare's *O Mistress Mine* with the modern setting generally sung on the stage now in performances of *Twelfth Night*. In the former, words and notes run happily, " coupled lovingly together," to use Campion's phrase. In the latter, the striking air of which seems to have been composed for the violin, there is no love lost ; the words have to adapt themselves to the tune.

Matthew Arnold in his essay *On the Study of Celtic Literature*, largely a work of fiction, has written interestingly of the Celtic Note, using the name in a sense of his own. He has been rather apprehended than understood ; and with later writers the meaning has become vaguer. This is due, at least in part, to the vagueness of the two terms, " Celtic " and " Note." I propose, in my study of the metrical effect of poems like *Cashel of Munster*, to use instead my term, the Irish Mode. With the rhythm goes a certain emotion, as distinctly Celtic or Irish, no doubt ; but emotions alone are unsafe guides.

V

ANGLO-IRISH AUTHORS.

IN the previous essays I have tried to arrive at definite conclusions with regard to the language of Anglo-Irish literature. Some questions which to many have appeared more important I have avoided, because I recognise that in attempting to answer them I should run the risk of suggesting more than I could prove, of drawing conclusions too general from very particular cases, of losing the little that I can hold by grasping either at too much or at other little that is of its nature elusive— worse still of begging the question, of running in a circle, of choosing the lesson to suit the example to hand. I have little sympathy with the criticism that marks off subtle qualities in literature as altogether racial, that refuses to admit natural exceptions in such a naturally exceptional thing as high literature, attributing only the central body to the national genius, the marginal portions to this alien strain or that. It may be quite true that John Keats owed the quality of his work to his half Cornish, half Welsh origin. I can say only that

I find it difficult to prove—as difficult as to prove, for instance, that a man of quite other extraction might also have produced work of similar quality. French poetry on the whole has lacked the lyric note. One need not for that agree with a recent writer that the French poets who have the more intense lyric gift must have been of foreign extraction. Less still need one agree that a great lyric poetry may not come to France any day and from the lips of French poets.

My definite conclusions are three :

First, that an Anglo-Irish literature, worthy of a special designation, could come only when English had become the language of the Irish people, mainly of Gaelic stock ; and when the literature was from, by, of, to and for the Irish people.

Second, that the ways of life and the ways of thought of the Irish people—the manners, customs, traditions and outlook, religious, social, moral,—have important differences from the ways of life and of thought which have found expression in other English literature.

Third, that the English language in Ireland has an individuality of its own, and the rhythm of Irish speech a distinct character.

If, with some of the best modern critics, we divide literature into poetry and science, the one to be attributed to the intuitive faculties and the other to the intellectual, it may seem that my conclusions have reference only to the science, the logical and the intellectual. That is not quite so ; but this work is itself a work of science in that sense ; it is a study, an analysis, aiming at the logical, at a clear intellectual grasp of its subject ; dealing with literature and language, literature and nationality, and the like, rather than with the wind that bloweth where it listeth or with the utterances, in terms of sense and wit, of mystic things.

It will be seen also that these conclusions bar out from my study the works of some Irish-born writers of the first importance, of Swift, of Goldsmith, of Sheridan —in short, of all but the more characteristically Irish authors of the nineteenth and twentieth centuries.

What then will the historian of Anglo-Irish literature have to deal with ? Who are the characteristically Irish writers that come within the scope of his study ?—What poets, what novelists, what dramatists, what essayists, what historians, what orators ?

The poets of the Irish Mode are evidently his quarry. Moore in the beginning is of them, Mangan, Ferguson. Callanan has a few good poems ; Edward Walsh a few. The best of the later poets must be reckoned under this head, down to George Sigerson, Douglas Hyde, and W. B. Yeats, the elder poets of the present day.

Equally within his scope are the explicitly patriotic

poets, many of whom have no other subjects than national
ones, and yet who have not in our ears, for all their Gaelic
words, the Irish accent of Ferguson. Such are Davis
and the poets of the *Nation*. Such on the whole are, in
our days, Gerald Griffin and William Allingham. Such
in much of their work are Emily Lawless and Alice
Milligan. There are a few poets, like Aubrey de Vere,
whose main work cannot be referred either to the Irish
Mode or to living Irish patriotism, yet who are definitely
Anglo-Irish. There are a few, like Lionel Johnson
and Nora Chesson who were born and who lived their
whole lives out of Ireland, and yet are truly Irish. Others,
whose relations with Ireland and Irish life were slight,
have been included in Anglo-Irish anthologies and the
like—Edgar Allen Poe, Emily Brontë, Arthur O'Shaughnessy, Edward Fitzgerald. The connection of some
of these with the subject is, however, too slender a link
to depend on.

Poe, who was a student of Mangan, had an ear for
the Irish Mode   Emily Brontë, on the other hand, seems
to have thought that the difficulty she found in conforming
to the conventional regulations of English verse was a
defect of power in her. She thought that to her was
denied, as she said,

> " The glorious gift to many given
>   To speak their thoughts in poetry."

And her editors, her sister Charlotte, Mr. Clement Shorter and Mr. A C. Benson, have thought so too. They have " corrected " and " regularised " her wavering rhythms, Mr. Benson changing " never " into " ne'er " and " even " into " e'en," and regretting that he cannot reduce " being " to a monosyllable. A good critic in *The Times* in defending her from these men of law, quotes an exquisite poem, never hitherto correctly printed :

> " Tell me, tell me, smiling child,
> What the past is like to thee.
> An autumn evening, soft and mild,
> With a wind that sighs mournfully.

> Tell me, what is the present hour ?
> A green and flowery spray,
> Where a young bird sits, gathering its power
> To mount and fly away.

> And what is the future, happy one ?
> A sea beneath a cloudless sun,
> A mighty, dazzling, glorious sea,
> Stretching into infinity."

" The poet of
> ' With a wind that sighs mournfully,'
and of
> ' Where a young bird sits, gathering its power,'

knew," he says, " the value and the music of every word she wrote and was in no need of assistance in the counting

or compressing of her syllables." What a pity it is that
she did not know, by more than an hereditary memory
and feeling, the mode of her kinsman, the Gaelic poet
Padraic O Prunta. She might in Ireland, with Irish
music around her and Irish speech, have come to confident
maturity, a great lyric poet. As it was she failed to reach
that confidence and that ripeness. " Emily Brontë,"
says the anonymous critic from whom I have quoted
just now, " with no dialect (such as Burns had) to isolate
and reflect her to her own eyes, was continually attempting the ' English poem,' unaware of her true vein."
So too with the other exiles and strays. We have to
share in their loss

The Anglo-Irish prose authors offer little difficulty ;
although their prose, except when it is a record of peasant
speech, has nowhere the distinct characteristics of Anglo-
Irish verse. The novelists are Maria Edgeworth, Charles
Mathurin, William Carleton, Charles Lever, Samuel Lover,
Gerald Griffin, J Sheridan Lefanu, the Banims and some
more recent writers ; the orators, Grattan, Flood, Curran,
Robert Emmet (by virtue of his one speech), Daniel
O'Connell, Richard Lalor Sheil, Butt and a few others ;
the historians of literary stature, Mitchel and Lecky.
The few Irish dramatists of the nineteenth century,
from Macklin to the foundation of the Irish Literary
Theatre, have little importance in literature. The

political essayists are Davis, Fintan Lalor and their fellows.

The names of these authors answer my question of six terms above. There is one other group of authors whose work is, in one sense of the word, more truly Anglo-Irish than that of any of the writers I have mentioned here, with the exception perhaps of such men as Mangan and Ferguson I refer to the great translators, those pioneers of Irish studies who rendered the Old Irish poems and sagas into an English which gained from the originals a distinct power and beauty. The importance of the work of Eugene O'Curry, John O'Donovan, Whitley Stokes, Standish Hayes O'Grady, can scarcely be over-estimated. With these scholars stands George Petrie. Apart from them, not a scholar like them, yet looking in the same direction, stands the strange imaginative Standish James O'Grady. The latest of the great scholar translators, Kuno Meyer, is a German, who, by his own work and that of his disciples, has added wealth of matter and grace of manner to the new literature.

VI.

THE IRISH MODE.

EVERY syllable of a word has a vowel and may have one consonant or more. The vowel may have a short sound, as " u " in " nut " or a long sound, as " o " in "note." A syllable may be stressed or unstressed, the stress depending on the pronunciation of the word, or, in the case of a monosyllable, on the meaning of the sentence in which it is placed In the classical languages, which had a full inflexional system and could in consequence indicate meaning without the same use of word order that English has, we may take it that stress had no real place, either formative or combative, in the making of verse Their metric was founded on the rhythm of long and short syllables—quantity. This system, in the case of Latin, was an adoption, but was none the less rigid. In English, metrical quantity proper does not exist, though English verse uses for a grace all the varieties of vowels, short and long, and of consonants and consonant combinations, quick and slow, light and heavy. The recurrence of stress marks the rhythm. The voice is capable of uttering, at one " pressure," up to three syllables but not more. That is, between two stressed syllables there may be no unstressed, one unstressed or two unstressed syllables. If, as in the case of such words as " superfluous " or " memorial," more than three syllables seem to be uttered at one voice-pressure, it will be found that there is either elision, as in "—uous" of "superfluous" (if pronounced superfl'ous) or the introduction of a consonantal *yod* sound, as in " —ial " of " memorial " (memoryal).

English verse, then, is accentual, a rhythm of stressed and unstressed syllables. Irish verse is also accentual ; but there is this occasional difference, that while what may be called central English verse, in order to emphasise the stressed, under-emphasises the unstressed, Irish frequently allows for the clear pronunciation of several syllables between stress and stress. Such Irish verse is not rigidly governed by the law of mono-pressures ; it is generally found in songs, the tunes of which have a good deal to do with drawing the metrical feet dancing out of their bars. This less pronounced hammering of the stressed syllables is more noticeable in Irish prose speech ; and on account of it English as we speak it in Ireland has a much more deliberate way of pronun- ciation, a much more even intonation, than the English of the English. One of the ablest living English metrists, Mr T. S. Omond, complained some time ago, in a letter to the

F

writer, that he could not make out the metre of a poem
beginning with the doggerel lines :

> " I once spent an evening in a village
> Where the people are all taken up with tillage."

An Irish reader would be content to pronounce the
words as they come, to read the lines as prose reads :

> " I once spent an evening in a village where the
> people are all taken up with tillage,"

not at all hurrying over or slurring " spent," "—ening,"
" taken," and not over-stressing " in " and " up."

Two examples from different stages of Anglo-Irish
literature will illustrate this tendency of our poetry.   The
reading of the first we know from its whimsical tune :

> " The town of Passage
> Is both wide and spacious
> And situated upon the sea,
> 'Tis neat and decent
> And quite contagious
> To go to Cork on a bright summer's day."

The last line of this verse is always sung in such a way
as to be almost spoken with rapid and even enunciation of
all the syllables.   The effect may be got by reading the
line with little or no stress on the words, " go," " Cork,"
" bright," " day."   In the song this effect adds to the
drollery of the words and the tune.

Very different is the well known *Lake Isle of Inishfree* of W. B. Yeats :

" I will arise and go now, and go to Innisfree,
   And a small cabin build there, of clay and wattles made ;
   Nine bean rows will I have there, a hive for the honey
      bee,
And live alone in the bee-loud glade.

And I shall have some peace there, for peace comes
   dropping slow,
Dropping from the veils of the morning to where the
   cricket sings ;
There midnight's all a glimmer, and noon a purple glow,
And evening full of the linnet's wings.

I will arise and go now, for always night and day
I hear lake water lapping with low sounds by the shore ;
While I stand on the roadway, or on the pavements
   gray,
I hear it in the deep heart's core."

In the line

" And I shall have some peace there, for peace comes
   dropping slow,"

it would be as wrong to mark, as heavily stressed, the syllables " I," " some," " there," as to scan it :

" And I | shall have | some peace | there . . ."

as some English metrists might read it.

Take the line frankly as if it were a line of prose, only
with that beauty of vibration in the voice that goes with
the fine grave words of poetry. (It is impossible to
mark the reading by punctuation or the like). Read it
so, and you will understand the true quality of this mode
in Anglo-Irish poetry   It is wrong to scan this verse,
to cut off the syllables according to the measure of a
rhythm that rises and falls sharply and regularly. Even
with some marks to indicate that though unstressed, a
syllable is slow and long :

"And Í shall have sóme pēace thére   "

the scansion is wrong. There is a recurrence in this
verse, but it is not the recurrence of the foot. I have
been able to take half a line to illustrate my meaning.
The first three lines of each stanza have a cesura in the
middle. I believe that that is the only division to make
in them, and that as a rule open to exception   In
general the second part of the line has a more obvious
recurrence of stress than the first, as :

"   .   .   of clay and wattles made."

Of course, as in all musical verse, there are contrasts,
exceptional first half lines that run with a regular scan-
nible rhythm, and exceptional second half lines like :

".   .   .   with low sounds on the shore."

This general movement, changing from a slow beat to
an easy rise and fall, happens constantly. I sometimes
think it expresses, whether in accentual verse or quantitative, the mingled emotion of unrest and pleasure that
comes with the break up of winter, with the south wind,
with the thought of the shortness of life and the need
to make haste to explore its good and simple joys—the
desire to leave the unlovely, mingled with a vivid conception of the land of heart's desire. It is the rhythm of
that fourth ode of Horace's first book. In the long lines
the four solemn bars, dactyls or spondees, are followed
by three light trochaic feet ; and the short lines, after
the unrest of one syllable taken alone, continue the
movement :

Solvitur acris hiemps grata vice veris et Favoni,
  trahuntque siccas machinæ carinas ;
ac neque iam stabulis gaudet pecus aut arator igni,
  nec prata canis albicant pruinis.

The system is :

It would be possible to treat the second line taken above
as iambic, but, considering the dactyls and trochees in
the first, it must be read as trochaic.

It may be objected that owing to the utter difference
between accentual and quantitative verse, it is wrong

to apply these remarks to the two. I have elsewhere
drawn attention to the difference, for instance, between
the dactyl (quantitative) and the triple falling accentual
measure of " merrily." This difference does not affect
the similarity between the contrast of first half line and
the second half line in both *Inishfree* and this ode of
Horace's For the rest, a rhythm may be produced
not only in music, in noise, in words and in other things
heard, but in things seen and things felt. And not merely
the words of verse express the emotion. In true poetry,
as the meaning of the words comes second to their rhythm,
and the rhythm expresses an emotion, it will be found that
the words mean the expression of this emotion as well
as the rhythm.

To read correctly Anglo-Irish poetry one must follow
either Irish music or Anglo-Irish prose speech. My
earliest conscious observation, and notation, so to call it,
of this speech was in Cork city about ten years ago. In
the house at which I stayed there were two children.
One was continually looking for the other and calling all
over the house. " Is Maudie in the garden ? " Jimmy
would chant in a most wonderfully sweet voice, lingering
on every syllable. Later I was delighted to note, when
living in a little mountain lodge above Rathfarnham in
County Dublin, that a blackbird which came to wake me
every morning in the spring sang just the notes of Jimmy's

chant—a blackbird with a Cork accent. One need not think that Jimmy was guilty of that sin of childhood never committed by the Anglo-Saxon Saint Guthlac, who " did not imitate the various cries of birds." Jimmy was not peculiar in his accent.

In such instances song and speech are not far apart ; and Mr. Yeats, for all his want of musical ear, owes, I believe, this peculiar musical quality of his early verse to that Irish chant which at once saves Irish speech from too definite a stress and from an utterance too monotonous and harsh.

At the same time one must not deduce from all this that Gaelic verse is a footless thing of sinuous windings. Nothing could be more clearly marked than most Gaelic measures. And these too have had their effect on Anglo-Irish verse. To do Mr. Yeats justice, since I have quoted from him to show the serpent, I shall now quote, to show the eagle, the Musicians' song from *Deirdre :*

FIRST MUSICIAN.

" ' Why is it,' Queen Edain said,
    ' If I do but climb the stair
  To the tower overhead,
     When the winds are calling there,
  Or the gannets calling out,
     In waste places of the sky,
  There's so much to think about,
     That I cry, that I cry ? '

SECOND MUSICIAN.

But her goodman answered her :
    ' Love would be a thing of naught
Had not all his limbs a stir
    Born out of immoderate thought ;
Were he anything by half,
    Were his measure running dry.
Lovers, if they may not laugh,
    Have to cry, have to cry.'

THREE MUSICIANS (*together*).

But is Edain worth a song
    Now the hunt begins anew ?
Praise the beautiful and strong ;
    Praise the redness of the yew ;
Praise the blossoming apple-stem.
    But our silence had been wise.
What is all our praise to them,
    That have one another's eyes ? "

This poem is really syllabic, seven syllables to the line,
like one species of Debhidhe poems in Irish—without, of
course, the arrangements of assonance. I do not know
if Mr. Yeats is aware of this syllabic measure ; but again
and again in his poems and in the poems of many contemporary Irishmen I find this tendency. Indeed I should
say that the effects of our more deliberate Irish speech
on our verse are these two : first, a prose intonation,
not monotonous, being saved by the natural rise and
fall of the voice, a remnant of the ancient pitch—a quality,

as it were, of chanted speech—and second, a tendency
to give, in certain poems, generally of short riming lines,
almost equal stress value to all the syllables, a tendency
to make the line the metrical unit. From the first of these
effects comes a more reasoning, not to say conversational
tone, which disallows inversions, quaint words and turns
of speech. Not conforming in our way of verse to the
regular English stress rhythm we have not the same
necessity as the English poets to depart from the natural
word order. We have not to manufacture a rhythm in
that unnatural way I take up the first book of verse
to my hand, the poems of William Drummond of Haw-
thornden, Ben Johnson's friend. The first poem I open,
the lovely *Phœbus Arise,* does not afford good examples
of poetic inversions. The lines, varying in length, go on
their way freely. The last three lines are a little flat by
comparison with the rest :

> " The clouds bespangle with bright gold their blue ;
>   Here is the pleasant place,
>   And everything, save Her, who all should grace."

These lines are a " regularisation " of the three that
ended the poem in the earlier edition :

> " The clouds with orient gold spangle their blue ;
>   Here is the pleasant place—
>   And nothing wanting is, save She, alas ! "

The reasons for the changes are apparent, as is the loss of beauty. But how could the poet have conceived the fear that anyone would try to read " spangle " with a stress on the second syllable, and to such a fear sacrificed his " orient gold."

The sonnet beginning " I know that all beneath the moon decays," which follows *Phœbus Arise* in my edition, will serve me better with examples Lines like

" And that nought is more light than airy praise ;

or

" But that, O me ! I must both write and love,"

would be read without difficulty and without that danger of wrong emphasis which Drummond seems to have feared.*

His lines are :

" And that nought lighter is than airy praise ; "

and

" But that, O me ! I both must write and love."

---

*An editor has declared himself in doubt as to whether Drummond was a poet whose inspiration was marred by learning or a scholar who owed his literary success to study. Anyone who has read his work will know a true poet in it. The pity is that he was not more learned, as learned as Milton, say, whose verse he anticipates—learned enough to know that true liberty is separated from licence by law, not sandwiched between the two.

The freedom of Irish writers from these inversions and from kindred artificialities and the resultant colloquial naturalness may also, as I have suggested, have to do with the newness of the English language here, with the fact that the people, whose speech is echoed in these poems, have no literary memories in English, that we are still at the simple beginnings, that our literature is still at lyric babblings. However that may be, I am sure that the Irish writers are more direct, more modern, than such writers as Robert Bridges, Henry Newbolt and William Watson, on whom have fallen the mantles of older English writers, or at least who fill their shoes

I go for examples to the *Oxford Book of English Verse.* I take, as I am seeking natural diction, a poem with a story and the living words of a modern man, an excellent poem, Newbolt's *He Fell among Thieves.*

> " 'Ye have robb'd,' said he, ' ye have slaughter'd
>   and made an end,
>   Take your ill-got plunder, and bury the dead,
>   What will ye more of your guest and sometime
>   friend ? '
>   ' Blood for our blood,' they said."

The diction of this, more especially in view of the admirably direct narrative in the stanzas that follow, is stilted and wrong. That phrase, " made an end," and the whole third line are born of pen and ink. Not so, though it is not yet common colloquial diction, is the language of Mangan's version of *O'Hussey's Ode to the Maguire*—to go back seventy years :

" Though he were even a wolf ranging the round green
　　woods,
Though he were even a pleasant salmon in the un-
　　chainable sea,
Though he were a wild mountain eagle, he could
　　scarce bear, he,
This sharp, sore sleet, these howling floods.

Oh, mournful is my soul this night for Hugh Maguire ;
Darkly as in a dream he strays ! Before him and
　　behind
Triumphs the tyrannous anger of the wounding wind,
The wounding wind, that burns as fire !
　·　　·　　·　　·　　·　　·　　·　　·
Hugh marched forth to the fight—I grieved to see
　　him so depart ;
And lo ! to-night he wanders frozen, rain-drenched
　　sad, betrayed—
But the memory of the lime-white mansions his
　　right hand hath laid
In ashes, warms the hero's heart."

O'Hussey is not a modern man, yet though Mangan gives him words and phrases that were scarcely ever colloquial, he gives him a natural directness that goes with emphatic speech all the world over, at all times. If this comparison be unjust, it is so rather to Mangan's bard than to the Anglo-Indian with his revolver. I have quoted these two poems for another purpose than the comparison of diction. Newbolt's poem has lines like—

"He did not see the starlight on the Laspur hills,"

which, contrasting with the beat of the regular lines, has something of the unstressed movement so often found in Irish poems. Here, one may take it, it comes naturally in the enumeration of scenes and sounds, as an escape and relief. Mangan's rhythms are much subtler, much deeper and more resonant ; his escape, as in the second of the stanzas quoted, is from precipitate half unmeasured music to a regular tolling.

For another parallel to the passage from Newbolt I take a typical passage from a typical Irish writer of narrative poems, Alice Milligan :

"'If I was home at all,'
She is musing now, ' I would go that way to-night,
I would walk that way alone in the care of God,
All doors are shut and no one comes abroad
Because they think the souls are out to-night ;
So in the windows they set the candles three
To let the wanderers know, ' We pray for ye
And love ye yet, but would look on ye with dread
Returning from the dead.' "

The inversion " candles three " is the only forced phrase in this

Syllabic verse, riming or assonating, develops, I think, internal rimes and the riming of monosyllables with the last syllables of long words   Of course the rules of rimes and the rest were never arbitrary   They were discovered. They are " nature methodised." The rimes are as accidental as anything in such a matter can be. The grace occurs first by that accident of the wind blowing where it listeth ; and then, being observed, the grace is sought again.   In Old Irish, syllabic verse reached great perfection   I give as an example the first stanza of a poem written by a monk, a scribe, of his cat :

> *Messe ocus Pangur ban*
> *cecthar nathar fria saindan ;*
> *bith a menma-sain fri seilgg*
> *mu menma céin im saincheirdd.*

It will be observed that the lines are all of seven syllables, that the first and third end in monosyllables and the second and fourth, riming with them in couplets, in words of two syllables. The constant rule in this particular kind of verse was that the second riming word should be a syllable longer than the first.

That is enough here about that wonderfully intricate thing, Gaelic versification. I leave it all the more willingly at this, as a certain over-insistence on its rarity has led many to think it the only virtue of Gaelic poetry. That such is not the case can be seen by anyone who reads, even in unadorned prose translation, poems like the dialogue between the King and the Hermit or Finn's Song of Summer or the Lament of the Old Woman of Beare.

Next to the effects of Gaelic metre and of modern Anglo-Irish speech comes the effect of Irish music.* The characteristic rhythms of Irish music are noticeable everywhere in the lyrics of the Irish Mode. In a poem like Ferguson's *Fairy Thorn* one can hear the notes of the dancing air—in the first stanza the beating of the feet to the music.

Note the different effect—the swaying with the wild sweet twist of the song—in such poems as *The Outlaw of Loch Lene* and Ferguson's translation, *Pashteen Finn*. I remember once hearing this latter song sung in Irish by a large number of people in the South of Ireland. The singers swayed their heads slightly in a slow, drowsy way ; and the song went on through its full length, verses and chorus, without a break. When I read the poem now, the original or Ferguson's version, I find in it—read into it perhaps—that continuous swaying. In the same way my reading of *Loch Lene* is affected by the way in which the air to the third line refuses to stop at the end, but having taken breath on the penultimate syllable hurries without a pause into the next phrase.

---

*On the subject of music and metre, see the author's *Thomas Campion and the Art of English Poetry,* Chapter VII.

So with a great number of Irish poems and of Anglo-Irish translations, imitations and original poems in that mode. We hear through them that music of our own.   I am no exception—who can be ?   Here as I sit writing this on a morning of spring, in a place under the jurisdiction of the Dublin Corporation, in a garden full of flowers and thrushes, a boy is passing on the other side of my garden wall whistling a gay rambling Irish dance tune.   There are words to that tune.   I do not know them ; but I know that, Irish or English, they have that rambling way with them.   I know too that some poet who hears that tune to-day or to-morrow is likely to be so haunted by the rhythm of it that he will lay the ghost of it by singing a song to it.

The earlier Anglo-Irish poets in whose work this mode is most obvious are Mangan and Ferguson.   In recent times almost everyone who has written songs and lyrics has it somewhere or other   It cannot be attributed altogether to the actual music.   Several masters of it have no ear for music proper, but this, I believe, means only that while deaf to the tone of the notes they are keenly sensible of the rhythm.   As Coventry Patmore has remarked, the tattoo of a knuckle upon the table will lose most, if not all, of its rhythm if transferred to a bell. " The drum," he says, " gives rhythm, but the clear note of the triangle is nothing without another instrument,

because it does not admit of an imagined variation."*
With these tune-deaf poets the imagined variation may
exist in a piece of music as in the rattle of a railway
train.

The most valuable and characteristic contribution to
verse made by the Anglo-Irish poets, by Moore, Mangan,
Ferguson, Hyde, Yeats and all, has been a contribution
of melody, a music that at once expresses and evokes
emotion. In the whole body of their literature you find
scarcely a true poem which, in the words of the book
reviewers, treats adequately a serious subject. Of course
this may be said of the purely lyric poets of all ages and
countries It is the epic and dramatic poets, to say
nothing of the didactic, who write formal addresses to
Light and to the Sun, who discuss at length the question
of immortality, to be or not to be, the question of medicine
for a mind diseased. Allusions to all these you will find
in the Irish lyric—more than that, sudden illuminations,
that illumination of knowledge which again is one of the
marks of the true poet—*imbas forosna*.

" Three things through love I see ;
    Sorrow and sin and death,—
And my mind reminding me
    That this doom I breathe with my breath.

---

*See the author's *Thomas Campion and the Art of English
Poetry*, Chapter VI.

G

> But sweeter than violin or lute
>   Is my love—and she left me behind.
> I wish that all music were mute,
>   And I to all beauty were blind."

When Irish poets write the new epics of this nation and the new poetic drama of the coming years, we shall, no doubt, have plenty of those treatments of serious subjects. At present a search for the like would bring us only the moralizings of poetasters, the obvious and the devious, the things so plainly seen in our path that they do not need description or indication, or so out of the way, so far-fetched, that they recall nothing in our experience.

VII.

THE LYRIC OF THE IRISH MODE.

FOR the present the best poetry of the Irish Mode that we can find is in lyric form, the expression of the individual emotion. Worth notice in connection with this are the frequent fine use and the frequent misuse of the dramatic lyric form. The form is almost as old in Ireland as poetry itself, but only modernly, I think, has it had the intense human thrill of individual subtle character. Early Irish poems of this sort are more direct ; they often begin with the simple announcement of the speaker's name, and then tell in those vivid nervous lines of the *dán direach* clear and simple thoughts of passion or emotion— poems that translate so literally into all languages that they appear almost too simple. The monologue of Eve published in *Eriu* by Dr. Meyer is a good example of this :

> *Mé Eba ben Adaimh uill,*
> *Mé rosháirigh Iosa thall,*
> *Mé róthall nemh ar mo chloinn,*
> *Cóir is me dochóidh 's a crand.*

Roba lem rightegh dom réir,
Olc in mithoga romthár,
Olc in cosc cinad romchrín,
Forír ! ni hiodan mo lamh.

Ní biadh eighredh in gach dú,
Ní biadh geimreadh gaothmar glé,
Ní biadh iffern, ni biadh brón,
Ní biadh omun, minbadh mé.

                                        Mé.

" I am Eve, great Adam's wife,
    I that wrought my children's loss,
    I that wronged Jesus of life,
    Mine by right had been the cross.

I a kingly house forsook :
    Ill my choice and my disgrace :
    Ill the counsel that I took,
    Withering me and all my race.

I that brought the winter in,
    And the windy, glistening sky :
    I that brought terror and sin,
    Hell and pain and sorrow, I.

                                        I "*

No poem of just that dramatic nature is to be found in
any collection of Anglo-Irish poetry, in any such antho-

---

*I quote and translate the first, second and fourth stanzas :
my translation is very close to the original. To indicate a
departure I translate literally the last three lines : " There
would not be winter, windy, clear, there would not be hell,
there would not be sorrow, there would not be terror, were
not I."

logy as *The Dublin Book of Irish Verse*, 1728-1909. In the first part of the book there is indeed no poem at all resembling it.   This dramatic lyric has had to evolve again in Ireland in this new poetry of the foreign tongue ; something of it has come with the language in which it is now written, something from the Irish through translation and transmission.

The opening poem of the *Dublin Book* is Goldsmith's " When lovely woman stoops to folly " In his book on Browning, Mr. G. K. Chesterton has an apt note on this : " In Palgrave's *Golden Treasury* two poems, each of them extremely well known, are placed side by side ; and their juxtaposition represents one vast revolution in the poetical manner of looking at things. The first is Goldsmith's almost too well known *When lovely Woman Stoops to Folly*. Immediately after comes, with a sudden and thrilling change of note, the voice of Burns— *Ye banks and braes o' bonnie Doon*. They are two poems on exactly the same subject, and the whole differ- ence is this fundamental difference, that Goldsmith's words are spoken about a certain situation and Burns' words are spoken in that situation."   Such too in general is the contrast between the poems of this representative anthology of Anglo-Irish verse and the poems at the end. The younger poets are personal, their poems are things " felt in the blood " ; their poems are not merely

poetical songs ; they sing out of the heart of the situation.
And it is with this very merit that the fault comes, the
abuse of personal, something which misses the justification of exuberance at its extreme, something which is
too literally expressed to be other than literal, and which,
if literal, is untrue. Within my limits it is impossible
without injustice to deal with evident examples. In spite
of all qualifications I should seem to generalise, to condemn some authors of this as a constant fault. So I go
outside and to the past for an example of my meaning,
and take a well-known English poem, that most frequently
quoted of W E. Henley's :

" Out of the night that covers me,
    Black as the pit from pole to pole,
  I thank whatever gods may be
    For my unconquerable soul.

In the fell clutch of circumstance
    I have not winced nor cried aloud,
Under the bludgeonings of chance
    My head is bloody, but unbow'd.

Beyond this place of wrath and tears
    Looms but the horror of the shade,
And yet the menace of the years
    Finds, and shall find me, unafraid.

It matters not how strait the gate,
    How charged with punishments the scroll,
I am the master of my fate,
    I am the captain of my soul."

This to many readers seems the cry of a strong man " in the fell clutch of circumstance " ; and when they know of the poet's sufferings and refer this to his actual life they admire it the more. I have talked with some who knew Henley, and know that they regarded him as a strong man with a great personality. But the poem, full of fine phrases and all as it is, is wrong and unworthy of a great personality—the poem thus personal, thus autobiographical in form, thus boastful. The poem, whether directly personal or dramatic, rings false. The strong man is strong in character and conduct, not braggart in words   If he claim for himself such courage and self-reliance, it is by way of protest and denial to one who has doubted these things in him. But a protest addressed to the unseen, unheard God—to " whatever gods may be"—is vain, not meant to be heard by ears divine, but to be over-heard by human. It becomes the boast of a vain man, useless so made. The poem I believe to be the work of a weak, conventional, self-flattering mood of the poet's   And it might have been so good a poem in another form, a tribute so splendid if written of another man, so fine an honour to the poet himself as man and poet !

> " In the fell clutch of circumstance
>   He had not winced, nor cried aloud,
> Under the bludgeonings of chance
>   His head was bloody, but unbow'd.

It mattered not how strait the gate,
    How fraught with punishments the scroll,
He was the master of his fate,
    He was the captain of his soul."

So in some of the dramatic lyrics of our younger
Irish authors the statement as of personal experience
and of personal feeling spoils the sincerity or at least
spoils our pleasure. I would not be taken as denying in
any way the claim of the dramatic lyric and the dramatic
monologue to the justification of imaginative rightness.
The poetic is rarely identical with the personal *ego*.
Good poetry is rarely, if ever, an exact copy. Intuition
gives more to a poem than the record of actual experience.
The potential lover, if he may be called so, or the potential
vagabond, being a poet, will write as fine love poems or as
fine wander poems as the lover or vagabond of experience.
If the lover or vagabond of experience do write fine
poems wrung out of life, still the imagination is more
at the expense of them than anything else—the imagination
and the interpretative faculty. For, once more, poetry
is an interpretation, an illumination, and not a narrative.
It recalls, it recollects in tranquillity, it suggests, it brings
a light, it brings a key. Born of joy, it happily and
spontaneously communicates gladness. Born of sorrow,
it raises sorrow to the crown of sorrow through sympathy,
in exultation. Poetry interprets by philosophy, wisdom

in great words ; by knowledge through the selection of experience ; by knowledge through the gesture of life, dramatic ; by knowledge through intuition always, the plenary vision ; by a flash of expression that a word gives, that a rime brings, suggested by a whim of the mind, by a dream of the night, by a colour in the sky, by an air of music, by a mute animal, by a chance word, by a word half heard, by a word misread, by a mistranslation— suggested by such, but suggested to the poet who is the *vates*, the seer, the interpreter, and then the maker, the poet who is the voice of his time.

Those of our writers who bring this interpretation to sincere words, narrative or dramatic, will be the voice of this time ; those who assume tones of actual record and then outrage credence will be no such thing.

My going to an anthology thus for examples is symptomatic of our critical attitude now. Palgrave's *Golden Treasury* has had a profound effect on the modern criticism of lyric poetry. But in the anthologies of Anglo-Irish verse we find the symptoms of another thing—the futility of culling and choosing yet. We have now two full-dress anthologies, the Brooke-Rolleston *Treasury of Irish Poetry*, made in 1900, and Mr. John Cooke's *Dublin Book*, 1909, just mentioned. In addition we have Mr. W. B. Yeats' *Book of Irish Verse*, a personal choice made in 1895, now very inadequate, and

Mr. Padric Gregory's *Modern Irish Poetry*, which includes only the work of writers of the present day. Let it be said at once that an anthology of poetry, especially a large anthology, represents the average man's choice—not that the compilation is in general the work of the average man, but that it is prepared for such. No anthology can absolutely please any lover of poetry but the compiler, and him only for a time ; no lover of poetry is average. Anthologies are of two kinds ; they are either books of poetry, poems chosen purely for the poems' sake, " the best though a hundred critics say so," or else books of poets, in part records of literary history or of literary development. Mr. Stopford Brooke in his introduction to the Brooke-Rolleston *Treasury of Irish Poetry* claims that such a book must necessarily be of the second class. " When the book was first projected I wished to include nothing in it which did not reach a relatively high standard of excellence. But I soon discovered that the book on these lines would not represent the growth or the history of Irish poetry in the English language." Similarly Mr. Cooke's *Dublin Book of Irish Verse*, intended to be final, exhaustive and representative of the growth of Anglo-Irish poetry, must be judged by this standard. Of its five hundred and forty poems there are less than a hundred that I should include in my choice of the purest pure ; but apart from that one must be glad that Mr. Cooke has included a host of poems that have other claims—the street ballads and the humorous songs and the swinging poems of nationality. The book is, up to Douglas Hyde and the older living writers—that is, as far as any book can be—final, exhaustive and representative. No compiler will again, I hope, go over the early part of the work ; that is so much definitely put in its place, and for that reason so much done for the future as well as for the past.

No such justification as Mr. Stopford Brooke has claimed for his book can be allowed to an anthology of contemporary verse.   Yet a book like Mr. Padric Gregory's would need even a better justification for its existence. Poems of little intrinsic value may have an historic value if they come early and prove to be originals of better work later. But contemporary poems of little intrinsic value should have no value to the anthologist. Mr Gregory has three worthless poems for every one worthy poem in his book, and so has failed to produce the good book that many had looked for. If his failure be a warning to others and save us for a time from anthologists, it may be well for poetry.*

---

*In connection with this subject it is only just to mention Miss Eleanor Hull's *Poem Book of the Gael*, a volume of translations from the Irish done by many hands. Though the book is full of faults, and some of Miss Hull's own translations

Poetry does not bear kindly the shackles of the anthologist : criticism is wronged by him.   He sets up a standard of niceness.   He sets up a false standard of clarity.
For the clarity of prose is not the clarity of poetry ; and
poets must not be struck dumb by the catch-cry, obscurity.
The true poet will not indeed be struck dumb by any
catch-cry ; but others may have their ears filled by such
and may be kept longer than they otherwise would be
from listening to the poet's word. " There are two
kinds of obscurity," writes Mr. Joseph Plunkett,* " the
obscurity of Art and the obscurity of Nature. They
may be called the obscurity of mist and the obscurity of
mystery. They have nothing in common. They are
as opposed as the poles.

  " A thing may be hidden by Art in two ways. It may
be overlaid with irrelevancies, or its expression may be
restrained to the point of poverty. The effect is the
same. The essentials are hidden. In Nature also
(but by Nature we mean not so much apparent Nature
as real Nature) there are two ways by which things may
be hidden. They may become so common as not to be
regarded, or they may be so uncommon as not to permit

---

are very bad, the book is a far finer treasury of poetry than
any of the Anglo-Irish anthologies.   It is drawn from the
lyric poetry of a full literature, though to us a literature in
fragments.

  * In *The Irish Review*, February, 1914.

regard.   They may be as universal as light or as unique as the sun.   Observation involves comparison, and that which is entirely universal or absolutely unique—or both—cannot be compared with anything.

" An artist is one who has the power of unveiling Nature, only to substitute the veils of Art.   Indeed it is by imposing the veils of Art that he is enabled to show the real qualities and relations of things.   For the veils of Art need not be obscure.   The vision of the artist is of such a kind that it penetrates these veils and thus can view the realities underlying them that otherwise could not be confronted.   It is through his Art that the artist sees.

" The artist's task, however, is to make others see ; for all Art is revelation.   This he does chiefly by the great instrument of inspiration, Choice.   He chooses the portion or phase of Truth that he is to reveal, and he chooses the veils that he must impose in order to make that Truth visible.   Here it is that the artist is liable to obscurity.   He is apt to lose the consciousness of his purpose of revelation to others in the overwhelming devotion that the vision requires.   Then is it that the quality of his inspiration decides the nature of the obscurity that is certain to result.   If his vision be powerful and his inspiration deep he will choose to scale the topless peaks of beauty and attempt to set down the splendour

of the spreading plains of Truth. He will fail to clothe
his vision with the necessary veils. His work will have
the obscurity of Nature. If, on the other hand, his
inspiration be more subtle and superficial, running hither
and thither in intricate mazes of wonder, he will multiply
veils on detailed portions of his subject, adding one to
another according as the various points of view and possible relations of parts come within his cognizance   His
work will have the obscurity of Art."

In his essay on Coleridge, Francis Thompson says :
" There is not one great poet who has escaped the charge
of obscurity, fantasticalness, or affectation of utterance."
With Mr. Plunkett we may ask, Is there one great poet
who has not deserved the charge of obscurity ? With
him we may answer that if we limit the charge to that kind
of obscurity that he has called the obscurity of Nature
or of Mystery, then to our knowledge there is none.

For the purposes of criticism here I would say part of
that in another way of the young poet. He takes for
known and seen by others things apparent to him only.
He begins by being the seer. He becomes the interpreter
and so the maker, when he learns to express the creature
of his vision as it must inevitably be expressed for himself,
and in a code known to others too. But it is better that
a young poet should have a vision and express it only for
himself than that he should have only the conventional

novel things worn by all the poetic of his time. He may set too high a value on the secret phases of his vision. The best is that which is universal. The poet finds himself when he gives himself.

And these obscure young poets are not all of one kind. Like many things that I have mentioned here, like all the men and matters of the universe, these poets may be divided into two classes. There are those who begin by being accomplished and come to power along the road which leads to straight simplicity, and those who begin by stammering, those who have slowly to master the craft. The former sing in well ordered words things known to them in all details, unknown or strange to others. The latter are obscure because of their incoherency, their difficulty of utterance.

I have dealt at this length with obscurity in order to set right in a little way that wrong trend of our time to discuss easily as obscure much very sincere good work of young poets in Ireland. In one other way their work is almost of necessity obscure to all but students of Irish literature and those brought up in the Irish tradition. To us there is a world of memory in these lines of Padraic Colum's *Drover* :

> " Then the wet winding roads,
>   Brown bogs and black water,
>   And my thoughts on white ships
>   And the King of Spain's daughter."

Others might well ask, Which King of Spain ? Why white ships ? and find nothing but suggestions of unpleasantness in the thought of wet roads, brown bogs and black water. I suppose one has to be baptised Irish to feel the right thing, as to be sure one should be baptised Russian to feel rightly all the beauty of Russian song, or changed into Chinese to accept seriously and simply the craft of the Chinese stage.

And there is the other great cause of obscurity. I have spoken earlier of the mystic element in Anglo-Irish poetry. Literature, and in consequence, criticism, have been so long rationalistic that mystical poetry is almost of necessity obscure to most readers. Most readers of poetry expect clear plain statements to have to do only with what they would call plain things, things known to the outward senses. If a poet makes a clear plain statement about any other thing—if he says that he saw eternity or heard the voice of God—which every heart must hear— or felt in his hands the fruit of the tree of good and evil, he is supposed to be poetising, to be saying in a hard way something that he might have said in an easy way if he liked, or else something that is mere nonsense and that should not be said at all. He is asked for an interpretation. It scarcely ever occurs to readers to credit the poet simply. And of course that is not wonderful. Since the old days of " Unknowing " in the fourteenth century, the English language has had little mystical use, and the terms of sense and wit now are good in the main only for the expression of the intellectual not of the intuitive faculties. Most readers will find it difficult or impossible to enter the world of the mystic, as in that of all worlds it is only experience that teaches, and experience cannot be taught. There vanity is vain indeed ; pride always has a fall. Every mystic has used things known to the outward senses as figures of the unknown unknowable with which the soul identifies itself in contemplation. For this he often uses that puzzling form, paradox : this identity, which is absolute knowledge not arrived at by reason, makes him know the unknown.

> " The middle of the things I know
> Is the unknown, and circling it
> Life's truth and life's illusion show
> Things in the terms of sense and wit
>
> Bounded by knowledge thus, unbound,
> Within the temple thus, alone,
> Clear of the circle set around,
> I know not, being with the unknown.
>
> But images my memories use
> Of sense, and terms of wit employ,
> Lest in the known the unknown lose
> The secret tidings of my joy."

It is for the sake of criticism that I make this plea for the credit of mysticism in our poetry, not for the

H

sake of poetry or of the poets, to whom that credit does
not matter at all   They have the illumination and the
joy.

The failure of readers has been due to yet another
cause then the mystery of these poets : I mean the
rather similar use of language to a different end.   Lord
Dunsany, who writes a beautiful imaginative prose,
wants to say that in the evening silence settles on the
earth, and is broken only by the cries of the night birds
and night beasts.   He wants to say too that the law
which governs this fall of silence and this breaking of the
silence of the night is a mysterious and divine law   He
says :

" And when it is dark, all in the Land of Tirboogie
(the Lord of Dusk) Hish creepeth from the forest, the
Lord of Silence, whose children are the bats who have
broken the command of their father, but in a voice that
is ever so low Hish husheth the mouse and all the whispers
in the night ; he maketh all noises still.   Only the cricket
rebelleth.   But Hish hath sent against him such a spell
that after he hath cried a thousand times his voice may
be heard no more but becometh part of the silence.

" And when he hath slain all sounds Hish boweth low
to the ground ; then cometh into the house, with never
a sound of feet, the god Yoharneth-Lahai.

" But away in the forest whence Hish hath come,

Wohoon, the Lord of Noises in the Night, awaketh in his lair and creepeth round the forest to see whether it be true that Hish hath gone.

" Then in some glade Wohoon lifts up his voice and cries aloud, that all the night may hear, that it is he, Wohoon, who is abroad in all the forest. And the wolf and the fox and the owl, and the great beasts and the small, lift up their voices to acclaim Wohoon. And there arise the sounds of voices and the stirring of leaves "

Now readers easily understand that It means a familiar thing, though expressed in an unfamiliar way. They easily believe that a mystic poem is expressing a familiar thing too, but in a way so unfamiliar as to be baffling. They think that the poet invents his images, not discovers. At worst they think that the poet does not himself know what he means or that he means nothing at all, winning confirmation from the poet when he says that he cannot express the thing otherwise, that he cannot simplify it into prose terms, that he cannot limit it to this application or that significance Lord Dunsany and writers like him make mystery in a gracious way about plain things. The mystic simply states some well-known mystery. He tells of God or of immortality or of eternity. He reveals attributes, beauty or knowledge or power. He shows the significance of some common things, knowing them as emblems and symbols of things and powers in eternity. He tells a revelation made to him of something like the fall of man. His telling may be difficult, but if it is true it will be in clear terms, and will be understood by many from the first.* Most of our mystic writings have been and will be in verse. The rhythm of verse is in itself an expression different from the too intellectualised use of words in prose.

One word more remains to say—of the importance, even the necessity, of translation in this literature of ours Some of our poems from the Irish are re-creations. This is due immediately to the difference of metaphor in the two languages, and fundamentally to that greater differ-ence of tradition, which is at once the cause and the sum and the effect of all our differences here. A phrase like " the star of knowledge " in Douglas Hyde's translation *Ringleted Youth of My Love* has a value that can rarely be given to such metaphors in English poetry.

" I thought, O my love ! you were so
     As the moon is, or sun on a fountain,
And I thought after that you were snow,
     The cold snow on the top of the mountain :

---

*The mystic poet indeed sometimes fears too easy intelli-gibility. " In the manner of your verse," wrote Coventry Patmore to Francis Thompson, " you are gaining in simplicity, which is a great thing. In the matter, I think you outstrip me. I am too concrete and intelligible. I fear greatly lest what I have written may not do more harm than good, by exposing Divine realities to profane comprehensions, and by inflaming popular esotericism."

And I thought after that you were more
  Like God's lamp shining to find me,
Or the bright star of knowledge before
  And the star of knowledge behind me."

The phrase thus literally rendered is unexpected and
exciting in a strange language of different metaphors and
different logic. The translations are in a way finer than
the originals. The " star of knowledge " has been used
too often in Gaelic poems to have that new magic now.
And other lines in the poem,

  " Like a bush in a gap in the wall
    I am now left lonely without thee,"

which are commonplace in Irish, have here a winning
grace

The literature of a race goes at first to the pails of those
who have previously drawn from the well of life of its
parent race. Chaucer is full of translations from the
work of his own people, the Normans, and from writers
among other peoples from whom his people derived
culture. Elizabethan literature is full of translations
and adaptations from older literatures in consonance
with the new national life of England, not from the
too Eastern or the too Western literatures. Shakespeare
" stole " all his plots and translated many of his sonnets
and songs. Later poets derive from Chaucer, from
Shakespeare and his contemporaries, from Milton. With

the exception of the returned refugees to the court of
Louis Quatorze, they no longer to any great extent find
their originals abroad. Our characteristic ways of
thought and ways of life in Ireland have been expressed
in Irish : other ways, which we have in common with
other peoples, have been expressed in other languages.
Mangan and Padraic Colum go to Arabic as well as to
Irish for their originals. All of us find in Irish rather
than in English a satisfying understanding of certain
ways of ours and the best expression of certain of our
emotions. So we are expressing ourselves in translating
from the Irish. When we translate from the French we
express Ronsard, say, a man of a different climate at least
and of a different complexity of civilization, a man who
warns his lady that her maids long hence of a drowsy
evening, carding wool, will start at the name of the poet
who sings her praises now, warns her that she will regret
her proud disdain while he, a pale phantom, will haunt
the myrtle shades. This is a different world, even in the
version of Mr. Yeats, from that of Raftery the poet full
of hope and of love, playing music to empty pockets,
from the deck of Patrick Lynch's boat sailing from the
County of Mayo, different from Cashel of Munster,
different from the Hill of Howth, " clear Ben above a sea
of gulls," different the whole distance between comfort
and the outlawry of our kith, from the world of that

untranslateable *Eamonn an Chnuic*, which yet we would all translate. The national rose of Ireland is *An Róisin Dubh*, the Little Black Rose, not the tender red flower to be plucked with the joys of life.*

At present a large amount of translation is natural. Later, when we have expressed again in English all the emotions and experiences expressed already in Irish, this literature will go forward, free from translation. Through the English language has come a freshening breath from without : with the Gaelic Renaissance has come a new stirring of national consciousness : these two have been the great influences in all new literatures. At that I can leave it, at that freshening and that stirring of it. It is well for us that our workers are poets and our poets workers. " The more a man gives his life to poetry," said Francis Thompson, " the less poetry he writes." And it is well too that here still that cause which is identified, without underthought of commerce, with the cause of God and Right and Freedom, the cause which has been the great theme of our poetry, may any day call the poets to give their lives in the old service.

---

*"*Cueillez des aujourdhui les roses de la vie.*"   Ronsard.

VIII.

IRISH LITERATURE.

WHEN canons of criticism have been drawn from the works of one antiquity and applied from age to age to all work of similar kind, when side by side with the " maker " has gone the critic and the historian, it is at least difficult for an heir of these ages adequately at once to judge the work of a different antiquity. When, moreover, it has become part of the common thought that the style is the man, when the work of a writer is, in the common mind, almost indissolubly linked with a known personality, a body of fugitive lyrics, the work of unknown men, cannot win recognition without very valid claims of intrinsic merit. Modern European criticism has adopted, with whatever modifications, canons drawn from the works of Greek and Latin literature. It founds its admiration on these works. In them it finds its touchstones of criticism. It has not broken from the hypnotism of their old convention. Example is the best definition. Some odes of Horace, with no philosophy and no emotional appeal, with nothing of the thrill of lyric singing, are still traditionally admired. The admiration is in part due to the influence of the conventional criticism, which drew its canons originally from work of the tradition in which the poet wrote, and which now applies these canons to that work. In part also it is due to the influence of the known personality. For in such a case the man is the thing just as much as the play, as much as the poem. The anonymous songs have their place, but the literatures, as literatures, are judged by the great names. To use again the example of Horace, we know more of him and his time than we know of the life and times of many modern poets. We think of him in terms of his *urbanitas* and his *curiosa felicitas*; still he may prophesy as of old :

> *ego postera*
> *crescam laude recens,*

for always we admire his modernness, a quality which may as well be shown in the interpretation of some ancient artificiality which has lived on into our modern civilisation, as in the expression of some old natural emotion of the heart of man. So we go to our Horace, so we go to our Villon, the scapegrace ; so we go to some or other " marvellous boy," some " sleepless soul." Consciously or unconsciously, we are influenced in reading Keats by the thought of his twenty-five years.

The Gaelic Renaissance is only beginning. It can

never be of just the same importance and influence as the Classic. It goes back to a literature of a different kind from the Greek and Latin, a literature almost entirely anonymous, a literature without epic or dramatic verse, a literature, as far as poetry is concerned, of fragments—little personal poems, nature poems, religious poems, short dramatic monologues and dramatic lyrics interspersed in prose tales. And yet it has been claimed for this remnant of literature, and claimed by the best authority in the matter, Doctor Kuno Meyer, that as " the earliest voice from the dawn of West European civilization, it is the most primitive and original among the literatures of Western Europe." Most original, and of not least intrinsic worth. It is a fragment. It must not be judged as if it were a fragment of a literature of the Hellenic kind. The difference between Greek and Gael is no fiction. In the purely Gaelic-speaking places, the people to the present day have their ways of thought and life different from the ways of Hellenised Europe. The knowledge and the influence of Rome and, through Rome, of Greece has not been unknown, but the matter and the outlook and the manner of the old poems are native. Native too is the reservation of the verse form for the use of lyric poetry. Because to say that the literature is without epic verse is not to say that it is without epic. The *Táin* is a literature in itself. The Gaelic imagination invented abundantly hero tales and tales of sorrow and humour such as others would have shaped into verse epic and tragedy and comedy. But prose was the natural vehicle for Gaelic narrative. In his essay, from which I have quoted (the introduction to his book of translations, *Ancient Irish Poetry*), Dr. Meyer draws attention to the fact that in later centuries, when the Arthurian epics were done into Gaelic, they were all turned from verse into prose. This, if it prove anything, proves less a want of power than a sensitive sincerity. Verse epic and drama would have seemed to the Gaelic mind as founded on a convention of make-believe.

The Gaelic Renaissance means to us not only the revival of interest in this old Irish literature, the revival of interest in the civilization, the culture and the history of ancient Ireland, the enthusiasm, the adventure, the pride, the satisfaction, the emotion that are quickened by the discovery of the old monuments, but, added to these, the study of modern Irish as a language capable of literature, the interest in the fragments and traditions that have survived, the reconstruction of our new state on some of the old foundations, and so, patriotism. A recent writer has lamented that instead of the Classic there did not take place in the fourteenth century a Gaelic Renaissance. Of course, the lament and all discussion of it is futile. I listen dreamily to it. To the speakers of the Romance languages, to the readers of Romance literatures, the Classic Renaissance was such as to a strange people, who had seen only the statues of men of our race, would be the sight of the living models. The remarkable thing about the coming of the Classic Renaissance is not its coming in the fourteenth century, but its not coming earlier The coming was inevitable. It was long prepared for. And when we use the same word, Renaissance, for the Gaelic revival, springing from the rediscovery of the ancient language and literature, and branching now into a double literature in two languages, we do not claim that it is quite the counterpart of the Classic. The old literature that was to be discovered, the ancient Irish art, were not in such consonance even with what of literature and art we still held, as were Classic literature and art with those of mediæval Europe, with the culture that still held allegiance to Rome and had memories of ancient Greece. Still at the heart of that lament for a Gaelic Renaissance five hundred years ago is this truth, that if history had been different the ancient culture and the ancient literature of our people might have had a more powerful influence on the culture and literature of Europe. The Celtic peoples had kindred memories with ours though they had changed their speech. Of Gaelic influence in literature, in art, in music, there have always been the sure marks and the sure effects,

as has been pointed out by Dr. Sigerson and others ;
but only during the last century has it come home and
thriven.

This is not the place to attempt a history of the Revival.
I propose here rapidly to survey portions of the literature
of ancient Ireland and to come thence to the literature
and the prospects of to-day. The poems of Old Irish
are from eight to fourteen centuries old. There has been
in the intervening period a steady enough stream of
literature in Middle and Modern Irish ; but my ignorance
of all but a small amount of this and my sympathy with
the way of the old time send me back to the beginning
and then draw me home to the new age opening now.

The themes of Early Irish Literature are many of
them the themes of modern romantic literature—in
lyric poetry, nature and humanity :—nature : the joy of
natural things ; the joy of the earth's beauty, the woods
and the birds in the woods ; the delight of summer,
season surpassing, grateful to dwellers in a northern land ;
the terror of the white winter when not a bell is heard
and no crane talks, when shapes are all gone ; the joy
of the sea, the plain of Ler, with its witching song, the
delightful home of ships, the image of Hell with its dread
tempest :—humanity : men and women, love and destiny :
humanity at odds with life : a king and a hermit ; a girl
who died for love ; a warrior who kept his tryst after death ;

Deirdre, the predestined of sorrow, winning some joy
from life before her fate falls ; an old woman who has
seen the passing away of her famous beauty, who sees
the ebb tide carrying away her years, who sees the flood-
wave foaming in for others. Later, after the English
are settled in the land, not humanity but the nation,
Kathleen ni Houlihan, is our heroic theme. The mani-
festations of nationality are symbolised by man and
nature. The silk of the kine goes lurking in the woods,
weeping down tears, while her foe has wine on his table.
The little shining rose is black. Ned of the Hill beats
on the bolted door of the Nation ; he is out under the
snow, under the frost, under the rain, without comrade-
ship, hunted with hail of bullets, desolate most of all at
the thought that he must go east over the sea because it
is there he has no kindred. No wonder that those
who, lured by the felicity of gracious words, have learned
to read with satisfaction in Shakespeare the easy hideous
history of the English Wars of the Roses, half won to
sympathy with ravening lust and barbarity, are perplexed
by Gaelic Literature of the middle period. And so all
Irish Literature is set down as vague, mysterious, obscure.
Nothing could be more clear, more direct, more gem-like,
hard and delicate and bright, than the earlier lyric poetry,
nothing more surely true to nature, full of natural piety,
nothing of another kind greater in suggestion, however

brief in form. Not till the advent of Wordsworth comes there anything like this intimacy with nature into other modern literature. Not till we listen to the voice of Shelley do we hear in other lyric poetry such prophecy of song as has come down through folk poetry in Irish, a lyric poetry which, as Mr. John Eglinton said some years ago, " has far more in common with the later developments of English poetry—with poems, for example, like Shelley's *When the Lamp is Shattered* or George Meredith's *Love in a Valley*—than anything produced by the wits of the London coffee houses."

The themes of the old sagas have been used by many in our day as the story of the Trojan war has been used by many nations that read Greek. Deirdre is to us

" the morning star of loveliness,
Unhappy Helen of a western land." *

They have not been used as successfully as the Greek models. They are not the inheritance of this alien civilization. They require different standards. To quote Mr. John Eglinton again : " These subjects, much as we may admire them and regret that we have nothing equivalent to them in the modern world, obstinately refuse to be taken up out of their old environment, and be transplanted into the world of modern sympathies.

---

* *The Three Sorrows of Story-Telling : Deirdre,* by Douglas Hyde.

The proper mode of treating them is a secret lost with the subjects themselves." It is possible, of course that, while I write, these *dicta* are being disproved. It would be vain, even if unluckily we wished it or could do it, to set bounds to literary genius, which is always breaking new soil, or rather always coming in a new manifestation. It is at its best and highest a new epiphany. Some in our day or after our day may make a great new literature in the tradition of this old world of Early Irish Literature. But I rather expect that the literature of to-morrow will be in terms of the life of to-morrow, and that the old world is too different, too far apart too much wronged now, I fear, by misrepresentation, by false praise that would make it good of another kind than of its way of goodness, by false blame that would call its culture barbarism, its strength brutality or impropriety, its mysticism magic, its austere sincerity in literature a defect of power and richness, its power and richness, when it has such, exaggeration. We may admit that we cannot now feel those old emotions at first heart, so to put it. We have not reverence for the same things. We cannot pray to the old gods. We could not blaspheme the old gods. We are of a different day ; a different light shines upon us. History is between us and our heroes. We cannot rid our memories of the glories and the calamities of our story, of the mighty things, of the futile things. Our thought is woven of the stuff of memory and elder thought and of a knowledge that has gained on this side and lost on that like an island in the sea. Our dreams are children dreams and parent dreams. A part of the old world lives in us ; to a large part we are alien not in speech only but in feeling, in sense, in instinct, in vision. We are true to the best of the old literature when we are true to that part of it which we inherit now in the twentieth century, when we discover in ourselves something of its good tradition, something that has remained true by the changing standards and measures.

I have quoted the phrase " the earliest voice from the dawn of West European civilization ;" but I should not like to be taken as meaning that this old literature is a beginning in itself, a first stammering, a simple babbling of simple things on the lips of a people just articulate. It is probably nothing of the kind. These pieces are but stray survivors of stray written records of poems that strayed down for a long time by oral tradition. They were written in the Golden Age of Irish civilization, during the sixth, seventh and eighth centuries. And even so only two or three poems have come down from those centuries in contemporary manuscripts. The records that we have are copies made long after. The language proves the earlier composition,

Here then is still another point of difference between this lyric poetry and the classic of Greece and Rome. And to point the difference we can take a parallel example from a different portion of the same literature. Professor Eoin Mac Neill in the Introduction to his fine edition of the first part of *Duanaire Finn* (The Book of the Lays of Fionn) has shown that while one of the great Irish epics, the Ulidian cycle, became crystallised and assumed what may be called a classic form in the hands of the Milesian writers, the other, the Fenian cycle, remained always modern, constantly undergoing reformation, always popular. For the full statement of this I must refer readers to the Introduction. To make clear my reference here I quote a few paragraphs :

" The Milesian writers, when they adopted the Ulidian hero-lore, adopted it as a classic, with all the extreme reverence shown by people new to any form of culture towards those from whom that culture is received, and by whom it has been developed. The Ulidian sagas, having once passed into the hands of the dominant race, became rigidly crystallized, and ceased to evolve. Most of the changes they afterwards suffered were due, not to invention, but to the limitations of the scribes.

" The early history of the Fenian hero-lore was quite different. The cycle remained in the possession of the subject races apparently until about the tenth century. As the Milesians, though masters of nearly all Ireland, never colonized more than about one-third of the country, the remaining two-thirds continuing in the occupation of the older races and under the rule of their native kings, it is evident that this epic of a subject race had an extensive public to whose sympathies it could present a strong appeal. Thus it must have spread from North Leinster, where it first took shape, through a large part of Ireland, ultimately reaching the furthest bounds of Gaelic speech. The period I postulate for this extension is the early centuries of Milesian domination, mainly between the years 400 and 700. During this time the Fenian tradition must have been purely oral, and therefore susceptible of local development to any extent. . . .

" It may be asked why, if the Fenian cycle was thus spread over Ireland, and accessible to the Milesian writers at all points, it was not taken up by them in preference to the Ulidian cycle, which, until the seventh century, was confined to one remote district. The question has already been partly answered. The Ulidian cycle came armed with the great prestige of letters. But a still more potent reason must have operated. In the seventh century the Ulidians were a free race. . . . A conquering and dominant aristocracy (the Milesians) would appreciate such a story of freemen coming from freemen. On the other hand, the Fenian epic was in form and essence the story of a vassal race. . . . .

" The history of the Fenian epic, as I have essayed to reconstruct it, offers an easy solution of several problems. It explains the form of the heroic narrative, and the peculiar rôle of the heroes. It explains the long-deferred appearance of the epic in written literature, and its forward state of development when at length it does appear. It explains also the almost exclusive popularity of the epic— its position for many centuries as the chief hero-lore of the Gaelic-speaking races of Ireland and Scotland.

" The legend of the Fiana, as it spread from race to race, was constantly undergoing reformation, and at no time acquired, like the Ulidian story, a classic and final form. It remained always modern, not only in language, but in the sense of being entirely the property of each succeeding generation of story-tellers and ballad-makers."

Do I take from its honour in holding that we have not in Old, Middle and Modern Irish a complete, continued literature ; that, excuse it as you may by the many good reasons of history, it is a literature thwarted and frustrate in many forms, and in the last two centuries or more a literature in decadence ? Rather I think that I hold a higher hope in looking for a new literature from now,

If the works of some of our contemporaries be not the first stammerings of a new literature that will have to go to school again, then they are the final senile babblings of one moribund.

To the eyes of criticism, Irish literature, after having suffered unparalleled persecution under the long terror of English rule, still suffers wrong even from its Irish admirers. It has in the first place been used as quarry by modern authors in English. The result, as I have pointed out, has not been fortunate. Deirdre, the subject of many plays, is an " unhappy Helen " indeed.

Then it has suffered criticism from learned people who do not know the Irish language, who cannot tell their stories as eye-witnesses, who are at the mercy of faulty translators, faulty philologists, faulty expositors, and who thus give currency to mistakes, mistranslations and misconceptions. The great name of Matthew Arnold will save me from the anger of other translators who have worked in the same field

A third wrong that Irish literature has suffered is perhaps worse than these, being akin to the higher criticism. The old Irish hero-lore became to a degree fashionable at the same time as sun myths and the like. Now new religions are made out of half-understood pas-sages of the old literature, India, of course, contributing whatever is not to be found in these. If anyone has a

favourite theory of the invisible world, he can use the
translation of an obscure old Irish poem for text. The
English words used in the version are sure to lend themselves to the vague suggestion needed. In a similar way
personages of the old tales are identified with gods of
foreign mythologies ; their strange acts and their strange
motives are made stranger still, losing humanity. Life
in some new redactions of the ancient sagas is not this
familiar way that we all know for all our differences of
tradition and literature, this way of love, this way of
wonder, this way of commerce. A poet of the Irish
Mode has declared that to Standish O'Grady he and
his comrades owe their introduction to Celtic hero-lore
The introduction then has been of a very special kind
Standish O'Grady is a poet who walks this earth as if it
were another earth, who finds and proves it another.
In him vision is more than sight. Such as he, in this
mean time of compromise and commerce and materialism,
may find it hard not to forget that all times are, for all we
know, equally mean, and so, equally noble—mean to the
low and noble to the high. Poets in every generation
regret the good times of a better past, seeing in the glass
of death only the heavenly colours that the blessed have
taken on, seeing sometimes in the glass of life only one
commerce of their kind, the traffic of dross and the
strife with hunger, and material utility in the mart out-

bidding the ideal. Such a one may forget or may not believe that commerce, even this one commerce, has not only its material utility but also its glory, its intrepid adventure, its strangeness and richness of far-off lands and seas and peoples, and so, its culture of wonder and imagination, its fosterage of the arts. Such a one may forget or may not believe that this one commerce is the business set over against the dream, keeping the dream true. The shop-keeper of to-day is the father of the poet, of the hero, of the saint of to-morrow. Standish O'Grady, too, searching for the ancient heroes, may have forgotten these and similar things, or may not have believed them. He is different from many who keep only them in mind. For the poets of the Irish Mode it was he that found the dún in which the wild riders of ancient Irish hero-lore were confined. It was he that let them forth, them or phantasies of them. Phantasies, some believe who have gone later into the dún and seen the riders there. The things that he let forth were viewed by alien moderns as Oisín was viewed by the convertites of Patrick, and by some that were pagan still. They were a wonder as they rode, and they sang in a strange tongue. The moderns who sought to set down in alien letters their semblance and their song told of vague romantic mystery about them The others who have gone into the dún have known of no such mystery. They have listened to their song in its own language, and they hold that by the poets it has been misinterpreted quite. The poets have used the frame of Irish story as a frame whereon to weave the palpable stuff of their vision and their interpretation of the heroic in life. Their vision is a mistranslation ; not for the first time has the world owed a beautiful thing to a mistranslation of genius. The original is a work of genius in another way of beauty. And yet for all that I have said here, for all their error of half-heard words, the poets may be nearer to the rhythm of the ancient song than those of us who spell the words in full. Some of the ancient tales, some passages in the epics, are altogether incredible and impossible to our modern ways of thought and life here. May they not have other than their apparent meanings ? They have the impossibility of the fairy tale. Perhaps they have the enduring truth of the fairy tale, of the parable, of the fable, which is truer than a history that owes so much to accident and whim and personality.

The characteristic qualities of the ancient Irish lyrics are those of good lyric poetry the world over. They have a simplicity which is never *simplesse*. They have a sincerity free from self-consciousness. Enemies of poetry as of truth are make-believe and pedantry and eloquence : essential to true poetry are sincerity and clarity. Newman defined literature as the personal use or exercise of language, for the expression, that is, of the personal vision or the individual emotion. Yet the vision and the expression of all but a few lack the distinction of poetry. The more distinct the vision, the more distinct the utterance of the emotion, the nearer is the utterance to poetry—granted always sincere distinction, not mere quaintness, above all not affectation or eccentricity. True freshness of outlook is rare in those who possess the use of reason ; it is lost generally with the first teeth. And it is not only " the light of common day " that destroys " the vision splendid " seen in early youth ; the hypnotists of convention throw over the eyes of all but a few a glamour of make-believe, and tune all tongues but a few in each age to their own accents.

As a rule posterity soon enough finds out sham in literature ; ultimately it is sure to do so ; but the hypnotism of a convention holds long at times ; the spell of make-believe is not always as easily broken by the voice of a child as it was in Hans Andersen's tale of the Invisible Clothes. Words have a tradition that gives them a price and worth in currency apart from their weight and their intrinsic value. Those Odes of Horace, referred to by me at the beginning, inferior odes, have in them well done what a long line of poets has sought to do. But those odes to a fresh mind, not under the hypnotism, would seem merely fine words well set, and not poetry at all.

The ultimate great test I believe to be the test of translation or transmission. " A thing well said," declares Dryden, " will be wit in all languages." The high things of the Scriptures, the words of Our Lord about considering the lilies of the field, are still poetry in all languages. When the language of their first expression is dead and the day of its most gracious felicities is over, they still live. If Shakespeare's phrases refuse to translate beautifully into some tongues, it is that their beauty consists rather in felicity of words than in high poetry. All that is great in his dramatic power, in his creation of character, in his philosophy, will be great in other languages, only indeed less great for want of that Shakespearean diction. On the other hand, some things, in verse, are finer when translated into a language like English than in their original, finer in their translation by Arthur O'Shaughnessy than in their original French of Sully Prudhomme, finer on an occasion (as I have shown above) in the English of Douglas Hyde than in their original Irish.

But this new consideration would draw me aside from those essentials of true poetry which must be re-stated before we can duly criticize Irish poetry—and re-stated clearly, in terms which may seem almost too obvious. How otherwise may one state clarity ?

The object of language is to express something. The

clearer the expression, the more successful it is. All the
great things of literature that live are clear, however
obscure to a passing age, even their own, blinded by
false knowledge. They are terse and sufficient, yet with
great lucid beauty, with the authentic accent of true
knowledge, of true feeling, of true interpretation. Perhaps the clarity of some of them seemed in their first day
a fault. A critic has written of the " terrible simplicity"
of Catullus. To some of his contemporaries the poetry of
Catullus may have seemed bald and obvious, wanting in
the graces of art. On the other hand, Matthew Arnold's
famous " touchstones," though sometimes examples
rather of felicity than of the high seriousness of poetry,
have all this clarity. But it is as unjust to take such
single lines as it is difficult to find a complete lyric poem
that has in all its lines the true accent. To go aside for
a moment, one may say that the little prayer to the Blessed
Virgin, quoted by Dr. Hyde in *The Religious Songs of
Connacht* is such, and such that old English carol of
the Nativity to which it has so curious a resemblance.
Though full of this gracious clarity, the two poems
are for the rest slight. The English poet plays with
a conceit :

> " I sing of a maiden
>   That is makeless ;
> King of all kings
>   To her son she ches.

He came al so still,
   There his mother was
As dew in April
   That falleth on the grass.

He came al so still
   To his mother's bour,
As dew in April
   That falleth on the flour.

He came al so still
   There his mother lay,
As dew in April
   That falleth on the spray.

Mother and maiden
   Was never none but she ;
Well may such a lady
   Goddes mother be."

This little carol is duly honoured in anthologies, and praised by critics as a matchless specimen of lyric simplicity, yet almost casually An Craoibhin quotes a poem as simple and as exquisite, taken from the lips of a fisherboy in Aran of Connacht :

A Muire na ngrás,
   A Mátair Mic Dé,
Go gcuirid tú
   Ar mo lear mé.

Ꙅo ꞃaḃálaiḋ tú mé
Aꞃ ꞁaċ uile olc,
Ꙅo ꞃaḃálaiḋ tú mé
Toiꞃ anam iꞃ coꞃp.

Ꙅo ꞃaḃálaiḋ tú mé
Aꞃ muiꞃ iꞃ aꞃ tíꞃ,
Ꙅo ꞃaḃálaiḋ tú mé
Aꞃ leic na bpian.

Ꙅáꞃoa na n-ainꞁeal
Oꞃ mo ċionn,
Dia ꞃomam
Aꞁuꞃ Dia liom.

(O Mother of Graces, O Mother of the Son of
God, put thou me on the way of my welfare.

Save thou me from every ill. Save thou me both
body and soul.

Save thou me on land and on sea. Save thou me
from the flag of pains.

Be the guard of the Angels over my head, God before
me and God with me).

This is a modern poem. Ancient Irish poetry has
many such pieces, though in general the religious verses
are more woven, so to say, like the Even-Song of Saint
Patrick :

" May the holy angels, O Christ, son of the living God,
  Guard our sleep, our rest, our shining bed,

Let them reveal true visions to us in our sleep,
O high prince of the universe, O great Being of the
        mysteries.

May no demons, no ill, no calamity or terrifying dreams
Disturb our rest, our willing, prompt repose.

May our watch be holy, our work, our task,
Our sleep, our rest without let, without break."*

It is in the little quotations and poems of accident, as it
were, that is least adorned that clear, sincere, colloquial
statement.   These for all of us express things with the
strange rightness of lyric beauty, once and for all.   In
the *Thesaurus Palæohibernicus*, at the end of the long
Glosses, one finds the little poem written on the margin
of a page in the St. Gall *Priscian :*

> *Domfarcai fidbaidae fál,*
> *Fomchain lóid luin luad nad cél*

The modern spirit has tried to invent in a manner a
personality for the monk who wrote that, interrupting
his copying or his study of Priscian to listen to the bird.
Doctor Sigerson himself, usually most faithful of translators, has added something in the last lines :

> " May God on high thus love me
> Thus approve me, all unseen."

---

* Translation in Kuno Meyer's *Ancient Irish Poetry*.

Miss Eleanor Hull in her book uses not Doctor Sigerson's translation but one of her own, ending also :

"Within my wall of green
My God shrouds me, all unseen."

There is no " thus " and no " all unseen " in the original. I give Whitley Stokes' translation of the eight lines :

" A hedge of trees surrounds me, a blackbird's lay sings to me—praise which I will not hide. Above my booklet, the lined one, the trilling of the birds sings to me. In a grey mantle the cuckoo sings to me from the top of the bushes. May the Lord protect me ! I write well under the greenwood."

This is the poem stripped of all its grace of verse. If the great test of poetry be, as I have suggested, translation or transmission, it is still exquisite ; but in Irish it has something that not even the best verse translation into a modern language can give it. Alliteration in a language like English is different from the alliteration of this. The seven syllables to the line of an exact English version would not have the fall of these seven. English rime would not give to the ear these rigidly governed assonances.

This little poem is useful to illustrate points of criticism, but is not a specimen of the best ancient Irish poetry, nature poetry. No other early literature has such a nature poetry, poetry so full of delicate, joyous observation, so wrought with delicate, light touch—

" Summer is come, winter is gone ; twisted hollies wound the hound. The blackbird sings a full strain, to him the live wood is a heritage, the sad angry sea sleeps, the speckled salmon leaps.

.   .   .   .   .   .

" The harp of the forest sounds music, the sail gathers— perfect peace ; colour has settled on every height, haze on the lake of full waters.

.   .   .   .

" Cold till Doom ! . . . . The fish of Ireland are roaming, not a town there is in the land, not a bell is heard, and no crane talks.

.   .   .   .   .   .

" When the wind sets from the north, it urges the dark fierce waves, surging in strife against the wide sky, listening to the witching song."

" It is characteristic of these poems," says Doctor Meyer, " that in none of them do we get an elaborate or sustained description, but rather a succession of impressionist pictures and images. The half-said thing to them is dearest ; they avoid the obvious and the common-place." They do better—they avoid the devious, the out of the way, and the thing of false imagination

How satisfying, how familiar, and yet how new to

us in literature is that wonderful enumeration in the colloquy between Marbhan and Guaire :

> *Mād fri samrad   suairc snōbrat*
> *somblas mblas,*
> *curar, orcāin,   foltāin glaise,*
> *glaine glas,*

and the rest.

"When pleasant summer time spreads its coloured
    mantle,
        Sweet-tasting fragrance !
Pignuts, wild marjoram, green leeks—
        Verdant pureness !

The music of the bright red-breasted men,*
        A lovely movement !
The strain of the thrush, familiar cuckoos
        Above my house,

Swarms of bees and chafers, the little musicians of the
    world,
        A gentle chorus :
Wild geese and ducks, shortly before summer's end,—
        The music of the dark torrent."

Of a higher mood than the nature poems are such pieces as that which Doctor Meyer calls *The Tryst after Death*, of a higher mood too than the justly praised old English ballads. It is a poem of the ninth century. The spirit

---

* Some species of birds.

K

of the slain warrior keeps the tryst with the woman for
whom he has died :

" Hush, woman, do not speak to me ! My thoughts are
    not with thee.
My thoughts are still in the encounter at Feic.

My bloody corpse lies by the side of the Slope of the
    Two Brinks ;
My head all unwashed is among the warrior-bands in
    fierce slaughter.

It is blindness for any one making a tryst to set aside the
    tryst with Death :
The tryst that we made at Claragh has been kept by me
    in pale death.

    .   .   .   .   .   .

Some one will at all times remember this song of
    Fothad Canann ;
My discourse with thee shall not be unrenowned, if
    thou remember my bequest.

Since my grave will be frequented, let a conspicuous
    tomb be raised ;
Thy trouble for thy love is no loss of labour.

My riddled body must now part from thee a while,
    my soul to be tortured by the black demon.
Save for the worship of Heaven's king, love of this world
    is folly.

I hear the dusky ousel that sends a joyous greeting to all
    the faithful :
My speech, my shape are spectral—hush, woman, do not
    speak to me !

Of one other old poem I shall speak at length. It is the *Lament of the Old Woman of Beare,* which one likens at once to *Les Regrets de la Belle Hëaulmière.* A detailed comparison of the two, however, would only show to us again the difference between the two civilizations.

La belle qui fut hëaulmière is a courtesan who looks back over a wanton life with a cry of :

> *Que m'en reste il ?   Honte et pechié !*

and then contrasts all her lost loveliness with the disgrace of her body in old age, and so, with other old women, regrets the past :

> *Ainsi le bon temps regretons*
>
> .   .   .   .
>
> *Et jadis fusmes si mignotes*
> *Ainsi en prent à mains et maintes.*

The Lament of the Old Woman of Beare, written five hundred years before Villon, has lines very like the French poem :

> " My arms when they are seen
> Are bony and thin."

But how different is the whole life of the poem, which is an allegory and a miracle. " The reason why she was called the Old Woman of Beare " (I quote Kuno Meyer's translation again), " was that she had fifty foster-children in Beare. She had seven periods of youth one after another, so that every man who had lived with her came to die of old age, and her grandsons and great-grandsons were tribes and races. For a hundred years she wore the veil which Cummin had blessed upon her head. Thereupon old age and infirmity came to her. 'Tis then she said :

> ' Ebb-tide to me as of the sea !
> Old age causes me reproach.
>
> .   .   .   .
>
> My body with bitterness has dropt
> Towards the abode we know :
> When the Son of God deems it time
> Let Him come to deliver His behest.
>
> .   .   .   .   .
>
> The wave of the great sea talks aloud,
> Winter has arisen :
> Fermuid the son of Mugh to-day
> I do not expect on a visit.
>
> I know what they are doing :
> They row and row across
> The reeds of the Ford of Alma—
> Cold is the dwelling where they sleep.
>
> 'Tis, O my God !
> To me to-day, whatever will come of it.
> I must take my garment even in the sun :
> The time is at hand that shall renew me.' "

All through the poem is kept the image of the tide :

> " The flood-wave
> And the second ebb-tide—

They have all reached me,
So that I know them well.

The flood-wave
Will not reach the silence of my kitchen :
Though many are my company in darkness,
A hand has been laid upon them all.

O happy isle of the great sea
Which the flood reaches after the ebb !
For me
Flood does not come after ebb."

In dealing with these poems I have avoided all reference to metrics. I might indeed have added metrical study of the poems to the things mentioned above as having wronged appreciation for the poetry. As I have said in an earlier study, too much ado has been made of Gaelic metres ; or rather, for want of due criticism and appreciation, the good metrical consideration has won undue prominence. Many in consequence think that Gaelic poetry is all a *chinoiserie* of intricate word-weaving, with no message that matters. It is sufficient to say that the verse-forms are full of subtle beauty, that they are of great variety, and that, as Eugene O'Curry pointed out long ago, the rhythmical structure of many of them exactly corresponds with the structure of Irish musical compositions of the highest antiquity. Of the old claim that to Ireland Europe owes rime I have written else-

---

where,* also of the nature of assonance, which is in Irish, as the late Professor Atkinson of Dublin University said, " not imperfect rime, but something far richer than rime, and admitting of a far more complex series of harmonies." I can the better omit consideration of this because the work has been so well done by many able hands in our day—by Meyer, by Hyde, by Sigerson, most notably. For the rest no one need fear not to appreciate the best of the old lyrics for ignorance of the rules of their verse. The one simple reading rule laid down by MacNeill in his Introduction to *Duanaire Finn* will suffice for these : " The reader of Modern Irish should bear in mind, in reading Old and Middle Irish poetry, that the modern accentuation of one syllable in each word must be carefully avoided if it is desired to appreciate the metrical value and rhythm of the poems. All syllables, in whatever position, and however lightly accented in modern pronunciation, must be regarded as equally accented in the olden poetry. Thus in the first stanza of the *Duanaire*,

Eol ꝺaṁ ꞃencuꞃ ꝼeine ꝼinn
ꞃe ꞃé coiᵹeaċꞇa in Ꞇáilᵹinn,

ꝼinn and Ꞇáilᵹinn should be read so as to rime fully The second syllable in Ꞇáilᵹinn should be accented as

---

Thomas Campion and the Art of English Poetry. Chapter IX.

strongly as the first, not lightly passed over as in the modern pronunciation. The same applies to all syllables in every verse, no less than the riming syllables. Again, there are no slurred consonants making one syllable of two, as at present pronounced."

Most of the ancient lyrics have been gleaned from old manuscripts here and there in Europe, written on the margins of grammars and bibles, or copied, a few together, in books of miscellanies. Some of them are embedded in the prose sagas, which are the most important reliques of ancient Irish literature. In addition to the two epic cycles, that of the *Táin Bó Cuailgne* (The Cattle Raid of Cooley) and that of Oisín and the Fiana, there are great numbers of other tales and colloquies. To learn something of the setting of the lyrics go to that treasure-house of Old Irish, *Thesaurus Palæohibernicus*, edited by Whitley Stokes. Read the introduction to the first volume, and all the end of the second. I do not know a more fascinating book unless it be the *Silva Gadelica* of Standish Hayes O'Grady, or the *Duanaire Finn* of Eoin MacNeill, or the *Buile Suibhne* of J. G. O'Keeffe, or some other of the volumes published by the Irish Texts Society. No mere description of the contents of these is possible. They introduce the reader into the old world of Ireland, Irish story, Irish poetry, Irish study They introduce him, too, to the work of the

men who in our time have brought great learning to the
service of Irish studies.   The writers mentioned hitherto
in this essay and the workers of the periodical *Eriu*—
men like Osborn Bergin and R. I. Best in this country
and a great line of University professors of Irish on the
continent, especially in Germany—sustain the high hope
and promise of the future.*

The future, however, from present signs, does not
seem likely to run on the wheels of old learning.   I pre-
sided this evening at a meeting of the Gaelic Society
in University College at which Syndicalism was discussed
in Irish.   The prose of the original paper on the subject
was a model of style, clear, free from all ambiguity, with
rhythm used for the purpose of emphasis—far finer than
most similar College society papers in English.   The
writer of this and the best of the subsequent speakers
dispensed with complicated and derived terms and went
to the root of the matter, making their meaning plain
enough to be understood by simple men.   To me the most

---

*Eoin MacNeill is professor of Early and Mediæval Irish
History, Osborn Bergin of Early and Mediæval Irish Language
and Literature, Douglas Hyde of Modern Irish, and R. A. S.
Macalister of Celtic Archæology at University College, Dublin.
The work of Professor Macalister in the region of Irish art
is of as great interest and importance as that of any of his
colleagues in literature and language.   George Sigerson, M.D.,
is also a professor of University College, but of a different
faculty.

interesting thing was the difference between the sentences
of these and the sentences of the other students, whose
thought is still in English. It was as if there were two
ends to each statement, as if the Irish thinkers took one
and the English thinkers the other. In English, voice
stress is necessary to the meaning. The emphasis may
be thrown to the end of the phrase. The better Irish
speakers in the debate this evening might have dispensed
with stress. In speaking of a recent strike one speaker,
whose thought was of the English order, said Do bí na
fir buailte (the men were beaten), literally, " were, the
men, beaten." One of the Irish order said Do buaideað
ar an lucƈ oibre (the men were beaten), literally, " won
was it, on the workers," or rather " victory was won,
over the party of labour." The speakers of the Irish order
said more directly and more fully what they meant and
they marshalled their thoughts in the more natural
sequence. Here then was a modern subject giving
opportunity to Irish speakers to express themselves freshly
and strongly and yet in the good traditional manner.
So, as I have said before, the literature of to-morrow will
be in terms of the life of to-morrow ; and yet it is possible
that here we may resume a broken tradition and make
a literature in consonance with our past. Our nation
is small. The deeds of a few men who see clearly, who
know surely, and who act definitely, count for much.

We can be concentrated into a little clan ; and he who makes music for his little clan makes music for all the world. The greatest danger is from our own criticism and from our own bilingualism.

It is unfortunate to a degree that while original literature in Ireland is still but stammering, criticism already speaks with full voice, almost too fluently, too loudly. It is more unfortunate still that this full voice should sometimes shout down the word of youthful enthusiasm and admiration. Criticism here is of European stature. It sometimes takes advantage of its height to push through the ranks of the ungrown and to issue commands from the front. Its proper place is the rear. It comes duly and comes usefully in the wake of other forms of literature, of lyric poetry, of epic, of drama, even of prose fiction, of the essay and of oratory. The fact of the matter is that this criticism of ours is an alien, an immigrant, or at least a cuckoo. An Irish poet, if he be individual, if he be original, if he be national, speaks, almost stammers, in one of the two fresh languages of this country—in Irish (modern Irish, newly schooled by Europe), or in Anglo-Irish, English as we speak it in Ireland, a language yet unspoiled by the over-growths of literature. Such an Irish poet can still express himself in the simplest terms of life and of the common furniture of life.

> " Her household motions light and free,
>   And steps of virgin liberty,"

sings Wordsworth, apostle of simplicity in diction. (I quote at random.)

> " She carries in the dishes
>   And lays them in a row,"

sings W. B. Yeats.

> " I look for ghosts, but none will force
>   Their way to me,"

cries the mother in Wordsworth's poem.

> " Mavourneen is going
>   From me and from you,
>
> .   .   .   .   .
>
>   From the reek of the smoke
>   And cold of the floor,
>   And the peering of things
>   Across the half-door,"

cries the mother in a poem of Padraic Colum's.

Of course Wordsworth has things as bald and as simple as any Irish poet could write ; but they are not the rule in his successful poems ; they are not always his best expression, his natural expression ; they are often the worse for being the cries of a conscious literary reaction, of a revival, of a return to simplicity. In Ireland we are still at simple beginnings.

And we are beginning in Irish as well as in English.

Compare with Matthew Arnold's " unplumb'd, salt, estranging sea "—a phrase English, modern, typical, beautiful—these lines of an Irish folk-poem, a century old or more, but still natural and of the same accent as the latest word of Irish poetry :

Mo bnón ap an bpaippse,
1r é açá món ı

(My grief on the sea, it is it that is big).

All this shall be granted to you, says a critic, but Irish, Gaelic, cannot go further, or at least cannot go aside from this, without violating the genius and the sense of the language. This Gaelic League Irish, says the critic, is full of awful barbarisms. Gaelic League, *Connradh na Gaedhilge !   Connradh* is an agreement, a league between parties, not a league in the sense of a body of people banded together with a General Secretary. The English words " league " and " covenant " came, in the phrase " Solemn League and Covenant," to be used of the organisation ; but we must not let Irish drift into that loose use of words. *Saoghal in Eirinn* is Father Dineen's translation of " life in Ireland," and he ought to have known better than to use *saoghal*, akin to the Latin *saeculum*, for " life " in that sense. The grammarian in me, the purist, approves of the critic crying this ; but another man in me cries : O happy Chaucer ! O

happy all ye who used words as you could take them,
testing them only by their current value !

And Anglo-Irish work does not escape. I hear already
the mutter of anger against the very name, Anglo-Irish,
and against the lines I have quoted from W. B. Yeats
and Padraic Colum. Just narrow peasant English and
nothing more, says someone—No, I wrong criticism.
The criticism to which I have been referring just now
has nothing to do with these opinions. There is a school
of criticism in Ireland, a school that knows the work of
the finest critics in the world, and knows too, what is more
important, the finest literature in the world. This, when
dealing with literature in general, adds to the store of fine
critical work. This at times encourages and approves
good original Irish work. I think it unfortunate, however,
that it should have grown with, or indeed before, the
original work. Dealing with the monuments of the older
literatures—English, French, and the like—this criticism
knows its place, its bearings, its conditions. Dealing
with a naissant literature or with two naissant literatures,
with literature still at the lyric stage, it looks over its
shoulder, as it were. Its neck is awry. Its eyes are
twisted round. Its feet turn from their known way and
stumble. When it does get a clear view of its object,
it misses the shapes and forms it saw in other lands and
expresses its disappointment.

Ireland is not the only country that suffers so to-day
America also has a full-grown criticism and a baby
literature. Something of the same relation exists between
the two there as in Ireland.

Of course criticism, this use or this abuse of criticism,
is not going to change what seems to be the natural law
of growth, development, progress, ever recurring. The
new literatures will grow in the due way, criticism or no
criticism. And indeed it may be said that the effect of
criticism on the author is quite negligible. Its effect on
the audience is not negligible. Growing naturally with
a native literature, dealing with a native literature in terms
of the life of which that literature is an expression, an
interpretation, an illumination, it is good. Coming from
abroad, full grown and intolerant of youth, it may here
be a false prophet.

Poets—and it is with poets we are most concerned
in a youthful literature—have in general to wait long for
recognition : those that speak with a strange accent are
not understood at once by all. It is a pity that the delay
of this recognition should be lengthened unnaturally.
The formulating of rules, even of just rules, the setting
up of standards, even of true standards, the preaching of
purism in language, the blame of innovation and all such
things, do lengthen the delay.

I take for illustration of this danger of alien criticism

a book of original Irish poems, published in 1914, *Suantraidhe agus Goltraidhe* by Padraic Mac Piarais. I do not offer my criticism of criticism here as an apology for the book : the book needs no apology. It needs appreciation and praise ; and on account of our present state of criticism it may go without both. I should like to clear the way for a new criticism, a simple criticism in terms of a new literature. I shall therefore merely offer samples of the poetry published in this book with the briefest of introductions. I think them good poetry and true poetry.

The book is one of the first books of the new literature. Irish has produced very little original personal work since the beginning of the revival, and the few good books that have appeared have met with an ungracious reception. As the adherents of the old Saxon mode must have looked on the English work of Chaucer, the adherents of earlier Irish look on work such as this. Written in English, it might well have had a sure success, like that of Padraic Colum's *Wild Earth,* from which I have quoted above. Being written in Irish, it is likely, on the one hand, to be blamed for having something of the note of recent Anglo-Irish literature, and on the other hand to be ignored by those who appreciate that same Anglo-Irish literature and who have remained ignorant of Irish. The book is not Chaucerian in volume.

It is one of the shortest books of poems I know : a dozen lyrics in all.   It is not, for all I have said on the point, so different from central modern Irish work as to incur the hostility of the purists ;   and indeed a part of its difference consists in its going back to some of the older forms of Irish verse and continuing them in modern speech.

The title, *Songs of Sleep and of Sorrow* (Lullabies and Keens), promises tender, serious poetry.   The note of the book is sadness ;   but in the most solemn poems there is exultation too.   For the rest, as a farce can scarcely be too amusing, too funny, or a tragedy too tragic, so a solemn poem or a book of solemn poems can scarcely be too solemn.   As I am writing in English, to introduce a book of Irish poems in which there is not a word of English, I am going frankly to use English throughout, even to translate literally the poems which I quote.   The language of the poems is so simple, the phrases so primitive in construction, that anyone who goes to the originals can easily, with the help of a dictionary, spell out the meaning.   The verse forms are so straight and so strong that anyone can know the movement, the beat of the rhythm.

Lullaby of a Woman of the Mountain and *A Woman of the Mountain Keening her Son,* the first two poems, are in the tradition of the songs that have come down

unwritten from mother to daughter. I translate from
the former :

  " O little head of gold ! O candle of my house !
  Thou wilt guide all who travel this country.

      .   .   .   .

  Be quiet, O house ! and O little grey mice,
  Stay at home to-night in your hidden lairs !

  O moths on the window, fold your wings !
  Cease your droning, O little black chafers !

  O plover and O curlew, over my house do not travel !
  Speak not, O barnacle-goose, going over the mountain
    here !

  O creatures of the mountain, that wake so early,
  Stir not to-night till the sun whitens over you ! "

The monotonous repetition of the one rime throughout
and the swaying flow of the verse help to make this
poem a perfect lullaby.

  With the fourth begins a series of personal or dramatic
lyrics. Some of them do not well bear translation.
Judged by present English standards, which are hostile
to sentiment, the mere words would give a false idea of
the originals. One, the shortest of all, runs another risk
in translation. It is one of two poems to Death :

      " Long (seems) to me your coming,
        Old herald of God,
      O friend of friends,
        To part me from my pain !

> O syllable on the wind !
>   O footstep not heavy !
> O hand in the darkness !
>   Your coming seems to me long."

Here is another of this series :

> " I have not gathered gold ;
>   The fame that I won perished ;
> In love I found but sorrow
>   That withered my life.
>
> Of wealth or of glory
> I shall leave nothing behind me
> (I think it, O God, enough !)
>   But my name in the heart of a child."

The last poem I translate in full. In English its title might be *Ideal :*

> " Naked I saw thee,
>   O beauty of beauty !
> And I blinded my eyes
>   For fear I should flinch.
>
> I heard thy music,
>   O melody of melody !
> And I shut my ears
>   For fear I should fail.
>
> I kissed thy lips,
>   O sweetness of sweetness !
> And I hardened my heart
>   For fear of my ruin.

I blinded my eyes,
 And my ears I shut,
I hardened my heart
 And my love I quenched.

I turned my back
 On the dream I had shaped,
And to this road before me
 My face I turned.

I set my face
 To the road here before me,
To the work that I see,
 To the death that I shall get."

One need not ask if it be worth while having books of such poetry. The production of this is already a success for the new literature.

In addition to this danger of criticism of which I have been speaking—an outside criticism—there is the danger to poets here now of too much self-criticism—a natural and good and even necessary thing in a mature literature. It brings a self-consciousness that gives pause to the impulse which creates, or which would create spontaneously without taking thought. Once the impulse pauses it misses its mark.

Then there is the danger of too easy a verse music. A language that is so musical in its words as Irish is difficult for the best verse. In languages like French and

English, prose phrases are continually harsh to the ear,
and words that sing of themselves are easily recognised
as verse.   This is one of the great advantages that verse
has in such languages ; it stands apart from prose ; its
words have a distinct music.   Phrases like A. E. Hous-
man's :

> " In summer time on Bredon,"

or Paul Verlaine's :

> *Mon Dieu, mon Dieu, la vie est là,*
> *Simple et tranquille ;*
> *Cette paisible rumeur-là*
> *Vient de la ville,*

or even Shakespeare's :

> " Light thickens, and the crow
> Makes wing to the rooky wood,"

owe at least half their beauty to the fact that they are
distinct verse phrase, however direct, not to be mistaken
for the prose expression of the same ideas.   In Irish
prose there is still the richness of open vowels and the
rhythmic fall of words, not so full and beautiful, indeed,
as in the verse, but yet not so distinctly apart as in the
languages from which I have quoted.   The quality of
form that most frequently raises Irish verse to the height
of poetry is not beauty of verse music, but re traint,
the severe grace.   A song like Seaghan Lloyd's *Bean*

an Leasa (Coir leara 'r mé ʒo n-uaiʒneac) is full of
rich music, with rimes and chimes and contrasts, but it
is sheer waste of exuberant melody on a barren theme.
Sometimes masters of verse-craft in the harsher languages
link words in this luscious way of sweetness, but their
verses are then clever achievements rather than poems.
Verlaine claimed, indeed, that this is the function of
verse—*De la musique avant toute chose*—and so, no
doubt, could murmur over and over with great satisfaction those beautiful lines of his which imitate the
sobbing of a violin :

> *Les sanglots longs*
> *Des violons*
>   *De l'automne*
> *Blessent mon coeur*
> *D'une langueur*
>   *Monotone.*

But these lines, gracious though they be and replete
with one of the sweet minor qualities of poetry, are no
more fine poetry than *Bean an Leasa*.   This exuberance
which becomes mere sound and a waste of melody is a
sin against the medium of poetry which is not chanted
song but expressive language.   True poetry always finds
its expression in beautiful moving words.   Its effect is
marred if empty phrases, however melodious, are added.
To take a simple example, the first two verses of the better

version of *Is Truagh gan Mise i Sasana* are essential
poetry ; the three that are tagged on in the song-books
are no such thing.   Swinburne praises a lyric poet who
knew " to sing and not to say, without a glimpse of wit
or a flash of eloquence."   The poet of these eight lines
had that knowledge :

Iṙ ċpuaġ ġan miṙe i Saṙana
   Aġuṙ ouine aṁáin aṙ Éipinn liom,
Nó amuiġ i láp na ṙaippġe,
   An áiċ a ġcaillċeap na mílċe lonġ.

An ġaoċ aġuṙ an ṙeapċainn
   Ḃeiċ 'mo ṙeolaó ó ċuinn ġo ċuinn—
Iṙ, a Rí, ġo ṙeolaió Ċú miṙe
   Inṙ an áiċ a ḃṙuil mo ġpáó 'n-a luiġe.

This is a perfect lyric, with the directness and suffi-
ciency of poetry.

" 'Tis a pity I'm not in England
      And one from Ireland there with me,
   Or out where the ships in thousands
      Are lost in the midst of the sea.

   The wind and the rain of the ocean
      To be guiding me over the waves of the deep,
   And, O King ! that Thou mightst guide me
      To the place where my love doth sleep ! "

The three stanzas that follow say the conventional things,
of a heart broken in a hundred parts and a dream of lost

love. I believe they were added by some one who thought the song too short, and who found it easy in Irish to string on the sweet empty lines.

A kindred danger that has beset the Irish less perhaps than the Anglo-Irish poet is that of rhetoric, the expression of the collective emotion rather than the individual, that which has given a small number of the greatest odes to the world and most of the poorest poems. The collective is in general enemy of true sincerity. Propaganda has rarely produced a fine poem. A great hymn, whether of religion or patriotism, is rarely other than the cry of a poet calling to his God or his country as if he alone experienced the emotion that he sings, though poignantly mindful that many felt it in a better day. Gaelic Ireland will have a great anthem when, in some great stress, a poet, using Irish naturally in all senses, will feel his patriotism as if he alone felt it, and utter it unconscious of propaganda for himself. The poet once again is his own first audience. His poetry is a matter between himself and himself. If others afterwards come and share his joy, the gain is theirs.

So much for the lyric poetry, or rather for scattered glimpses of it far and near. I have not, of course, attempted to do more than indicate points of interest and significance. Every century has had its poets and its schools and its movements. Of lyric poetry there has been a constant, though at times a narrow stream.   The libraries of Europe are still giving up stores of poetry long forgotten.   Old men and women all round the Gaelic crescent of Ireland are still telling out lovely lyrics of known and unknown authorship.   The quest of such is adventurous and romantic, only less so perhaps than the quest of living but forgotten poets or of the traces of poets once of great fame in their clan and still remembered by the living.   Douglas Hyde has been able to discover not only the poems of Raftery, whose word seemed a wandering voice far off, but a man who assisted at his burial, and a whole body of tradition about him.   Mr. P. H. Pearse and others who undertook the publication of the poems of Colm Wallace, were able a few years ago to discover not only the work, but the man himself, thought dead for many years but actually living, a centenarian in Oughterard workhouse.*   Robert Weldon, the poet of the Comeraghs, seemed to us in Dublin some years ago like a visitant from the old Gaelic world.

So much for the poetry

Of the novel and the modern essay, of which we have had many examples of late, I dare not speak.   Irish prose

---

*Mr. Pearse's committee took the poet out of the workhouse, but subsequently had to let him return to it as a paying patient at his urgent request.   He died at the age of a hundred and ten.

I believe to be a finer vehicle than English prose. The poise and the concision of the idiomatic Irish sentence makes our long series of words in English seem weak by comparison. But that is a matter of language. Of the actual work of the acknowledged master of Modern Irish prose, Canon Peter O'Leary, one does not know well what to think. His novels and his plays should not be subjected to this outside criticism. Of his use of his medium and of his descriptive power one can write nothing but praise and quote examples which must suffice for all. I give a translation of a passage from his novel *Seadna*, as more representative of the new literature than his sermons, his plays, or his adaptations of old tales.

It was a wedding feast. One of the pipers knew the Fairy Music. He would often play it to himself; but it was very hard to make him play it when asked by others. He said that it was not right to play it in the presence of mortals—it was too eerie. On this occasion, after much pressing by all the guests, the piper drank some of the wine of the king and consented to play the Fairy Music.

" He tuned his pipes. He filled the bag with air. The company listened as though they had neither soul nor breath. Soon there was heard, as it were, a soft, murmuring sound, circling the house without. Then the people thought a breeze was blowing, with the murmur-

ing, and that it was the breeze which caused the murmuring and not the pipes. Thereafter passed a pleasant
melody through the murmuring, and both melody and
murmuring came into the house. The murmuring increased, and there arose, as it were, a trembling and a
swaying in its sound. Soon a second sound was heard,
trembling and swaying like the first, whilst the sweet
melody was heard through them both, none of the three
obscuring either of the other two, but each of the three
aiding the others, so that the melody was the better for
the murmurings and the murmurings all the sweeter
for the melody. Anon there spoke a third sound, trembling and swaying with pleasant music through it of its
own. That third sound startled all who were there.
They would swear it was a human voice.

" Then came as it were a torrent of melody, the most
delicious, the sweetest, the gentlest, the most soothing
that the people there had ever heard, and it mingled with
the murmurings and with the sound like the human
voice and the sound that was like the blowing of the
breeze, and all the elements commingled began to move
around the house like a whirlwind. The sound kept
increasing in volume, the union of its parts grew closer
and closer, and the revolutions about the house became
ever faster, until the people thought that the fairy blast
was whirling about the house. It was now here, now

there. It would spring away and leap back again. It would lie down close to the ground and sweep around beneath the floor. Then, with a bound, it was on high playing amongst the rafters, in such wise that the people thought they heard the beating of birds' wings through the music. Now the people believed they heard the sobbing of one in tears, and anon bursts of laughter. Again they thought they heard plainly, speaking through the music, the voice of a child. Then came another childlike voice to answer it, and both made answer to the melody. Then there spoke a third voice, as it were the voice of a young woman, but none of those who were there ever heard human voice so sweet, so beautiful, so pleasing. Soon another woman-voice came to answer it, and if the first was sweet, the second was sweeter far, and they kept speaking to each other and to the music in tuneful measure. Then, as though some door were flung open, there came a swelling, a rising, and a strength into all the music. The movement grew faster, its rush increased, and a flood of joy poured into the notes. They rose and fell. They were below on the ground and above in the rafters, in this corner and in that, till fear began to creep over the people as they cast hasty glances over their shoulders to see if anyone had spoken.

" Then the music increased yet more in strength, as though another door wider than the first had been flung

open. Still greater grew the swelling and the verve of
the music, as it twisted and writhed about the floor and
over the walls and away up to the highest ridge of the
ceiling, now lowing, now crying out, now weeping
aloud, now wailing with grief, in such wise that it would
cause even a stone to sob ; now exploding in bursts of
mirthful laughter, now bursting into cries of pride and
power, so that one would think it could raise the dead
from the clay. There were voices of women and children, talking and answering clearly, through the cries
that were loudest, through the grief that was saddest,
through the laughter that was merriest. And ever and
anon through all the maze, there would come a long-
drawn, strange, cruel cry, that sent the shudder of fear
through all in the house. And by-and-by came the
muttering of thunder, rising and falling and rumbling,
swaying and trembling. It went through the beams of
the house, through the wood of the chairs, and through
the bones of the people. It grew and grew in strength
till it gathered to itself all the other sounds and swept
them with it round the house like straws in a whirlpool.
Ever louder and heavier grew the thunder, spinning
round with increasing force, swaying and vibrating ever
more through the timbers and through the people's
limbs, until every heart was throbbing fast and every
head was dizzy.

" Then the child-voice passed away through the chimney, and then the woman-voice followed, and so with each other sound in the music, till naught was left of all but the thunder still rocking and trembling. Then the thunder grew less loud. Its swaying and trembling grew ever weaker, and its rush ever feebler. Its strength faded away till there was left of it but a murmur. The murmur died down till there was left of it but a breathing. And then it ceased.

" Then the cock crew, and Báb of the Liss uttering a piercing cry fell down in a faint.

" No one stirred. You would think that they sat enchanted. But at last the Big Tinker jumped up.

" ' Arrah, praises be to God ! ' said he, ' what's on ye ? Come, women, two of you take hold of the girl, and carry her out in the air.' "

In drama, for all our efforts these ten or fifteen years, we are still waiting for a fine work, stronger and more enduring than such good little plays as Douglas Hyde's *An Naomh ar Iarraidh,* and *An Tinceir agus an tSidheog.* An organisation like the Gaelic League is scarcely calculated to produce literature. I believe that it would be better for Ireland and for the Irish language if, instead of the Gaelic League as it is, we had a different thing, a folk movement in the Gaedhealtacht, a movement coming

from the West eastward, not an organisation with the
official institutions of a political propagandist society, with
its capital the capital of the Pale.   It would, no doubt,
be better still to have both things, the folk movement
and the League, but there is little chance of that.   I do
not think that my criticism or the criticism of others will
now make the Gaelic League reform itself, and set about
work in a different way, yet my criticism is not factious,
as it would be if I thought that nothing might possibly
come of it.   The workers in the Gaelic League do the
work to their hand ; but they do little to foster the growth
of a new literature in Irish.   Most of us agree that if
modern Irish had a fine literature—fine poetry, fine
drama—very many who are not now seriously affected
by the propagandist appeals to them to learn Irish would
do so, not because it has patriotic claims or grammatical
or philological claims, but in order to read and know
Irish literature, as they learn Italian to read Dante and
Carducci, or German to read Goethe and Heine—as
some have learned the languages of Mistral and Ibsen to
read and understand those writers at their true best.   Mr.
George Moore has said that if he had learned Irish the
language would probably now be saved, as he might have
written such masterpieces in Irish as readers in this and
other countries could not neglect to study in their original
versions.   Even with knowledge of Mr. Moore's work,

and with the example of Mistral before me, I am not certain that alone he could have done all that, but his idea
is a right idea.   If a language have a good literature, it is
certain to be recognised and to have students.   Now the
Gaelic League does little to foster the production of such
a literature ; it tries to do much, but fails.   In the cir-
cumstances it could not but fail.   Since I have been
interested in Irish I have come to see the possibility of
truth in Gray's line about a " mute inglorious Milton."
I had learned to believe that as all men now have as
much chance of acquiring the culture from which literature
comes as Burns had, and as some of the ancient writers
had, genius would out.   There are no rules for genius,
but still there is force in that thought of Gray's, a force
that weakens the argument in which I believed.   Burns
had   behind   him   all   the   tradition of Lowland Scots
literature, freshened by acquaintance with Shakespeare
and the great writers of English, which is really the same
language.   So with the ancients in their different age—
I will not now labour the points of difference.   But the
people of the Gaedhealtacht have no models except the
out-worn verse-forms of the later Irish poets, and such
English literature as comes their way.   In Ireland at present this model should be the drama, and the Gaelic
League could, I believe, by giving dramatic models to
young Irish writers, do more even towards making Irish

attractive to English speakers and foreigners, than by
giving many prizes at the Oireachtas for all sorts of essays
and stories and plays.   This would be doing the work
indirectly, no doubt, but would be the better way in the
long run.   As Mr. W. B. Yeats has shown, drama as the
right form to foster.   Writing in *Samhain* in 1904, Mr.
Yeats said : " There are two kinds of poetry, and they
are co-mingled in all the greatest works.   When the tide
of life sinks low there are pictures, as in the *Ode on
a Grecian Urn*, and in Virgil at the plucking of the
Golden Bough.   The pictures make us sorrowful.   We
share the poet's separation from what he describes.   It
is life in the mirror, and our desire for it is as the
desire of the lost souls for God.   But when Lucifer stands
among his friends, when Villon sings his dead ladies to so
gallant a rhythm, when Timon makes his epitaph, we feel
no sorrow, for life herself has made one of her eternal
gestures, has called up into our hearts her energy that is
eternal delight.   In Ireland, where the tide of life is
rising, we turn, not to picture-making but to the
imagination of personality—to drama, gesture."

The new Gaelic literature might have its centre in the
drama. The drama may be a graft on the Gaelic tree, but
that tree is all but barren now, and we want new fruit.
In order to found and to foster a dramatic literature
in Gaelic it is necessary to teach young writers what the

drama is. One cannot, with all the good will and all the good money in the world, produce literature to order, but one can lay down canons of criticism, one can strive to keep the way clear for the coming of a good thing by correcting false impressions, and—what is more to the point in this matter—one can set up good models and display them, when the models are at hand and the pedestals empty.

Canons of criticism are not brain-spun and merely theoretic; they are, or should be, drawn from master-pieces. There are certain qualities in all true art, in all fine poetry, in all good drama. Writers of plays in Irish want to produce dramas of a certain kind—very distinctively Irish, very characteristic in the right sense, but still of the same kind as certain plays in other languages—to take the example nearest home, as certain plays about Ireland written in English. They want to produce such dramas, but they have not studied the models which have been followed by the writers of the plays in English. They have done little or nothing towards mastering their craft, and they have failed in their endeavour.

The pedestals on which the models may be set are empty. Judging from all but one of the plays sent in for the Oireachtas some years ago, when I was adjudicator, the authors have no conception of what a play is. It

M

is unfortunate that the one exception, which was the work of a man who does understand the craft, and was in every way admirable, was of a cosmopolitan description, not at all so Gaelic in character as several plays written in English. The others were for the most part stories or essays written in the form of dialogues or catechisms. They had no dramatic sequence or balance. The situations did not flow from the characters, as they do inevitably in all good drama. There is such a thing as stage-craft. The dramatist must learn his craft as a dramatist over and above his craft as a writer, and before he begins he must have in him the makings of a dramatist and a conception of dramatic art. I believe that the people to whom we must look to produce a new Irish literature are young people of the Gaedhealtacht, not people who have lost their Gaelic edge in the Pale. I believe that there are enough young Gaelic writers of dramatic talent to make the beginnings of a distinguished dramatic literature in Irish. The difficulty is to make them master the craft.

If a small company of Irish-speaking actors were sent by the Gaelic League to take four or five very well written, well constructed plays (one-act plays to begin with) from village to village in the most Irish-speaking districts, I am sure that within a year we should have the beginning of a real Gaelic dramatic literature. Visits of a Gaelic company would have immediate results. For plays to send on tour one would use the best of the plays already written and translations of the most Irish pieces of the Abbey Theatre—a tragedy, say, a merry comedy and a serious comedy. Farce is too easy and sets our young writers on a false track. I do not think that a group of players from Dublin or elsewhere, going down to some villages in holiday time, would achieve the object proposed. The actors should be well trained and should form a professional company, playing again and again in each village. The method of Molière is the true method, and brings drama home at last to the house of Molière. A folk movement in the Gaedhealtacht would certainly have given us a distinctive literature : now this touring company would stir the waters.

To this it may be objected that in our age literature is metropolitan—that it will have its centre not only in the drama but in the city playhouse. But if we are seeking the expression in Gaelic literature of the Gaelic ways of thought and life we shall have to draw it from the Gaedhealtacht. It will, as I have said, come home to the city playhouse after. The necessity for drawing speedily what we can of that expression now is clear to those of us who know at first hand how the old oral tradition is dying, who have known poets and shanachies full of

Gaelic lore to die with all their treasures in their hearts, leaving no records and no succession. Some years ago in West Cork I spent a day with such a one, an old man who knew more poems, more hero-tales, more biographical tales of the Munster Bards than he ever had a chance of saying or telling. When I brought him a copy of the works of Eoghan Ruadh O Suilleabháin, he was able to explain passage after passage, reference after reference, in terms of this tradition of his. He was able to detect the passages and poems wrongly attributed to the poet. " That's not by Eoghan Ruadh. That was written by Mary O'Shea, from Carriganimy beyond. I learned it for a wedding forty years ago. This is it, isn't it ? " He sang the poem, many verses of it, to a monotonous tune, marking the emphatic points by slapping my knee. My knowledge of Irish at the time and my patience of the music were soon exhausted, and I fear I discouraged the splendid old man, whom I never saw again. His children, though interested in the revival of the Irish language, are not heirs to his tradition. With him has died a whole store of literature and idiom.

As to the value of such a store I have no doubt. The Irish writer who is probably greatest of our time, that strong, self-sufficing, humorous, wise, old priest, whose prose I have quoted, has told me that in his version of the New Testament he was aided by his memory of sermons and impromptu translations made by Irish-speaking priests of half a century ago. Irish recently tended to meet English half way. The order of phrases tended to change. Writers tended to express things in the English order rather than in the Irish—worse still, tended to translate the English or French words for a thought rather than to express the thought in the different Gaelic way. Their prose resembled a certain kind of schoolboy Latin, a close translation, phrase by phrase of an English passage, possible phrase by phrase in another sense, but not a Latin rendering of the thought, not Latin prose. These tendencies were bad. By Canon O'Leary and others they have been checked. Writers have been sent back to the well of tradition and of the living speech. Drama must go to that well too. And it will go. For all that I have written of the wreck and ruin going on so rapidly, I am confident of the future. Many of us are good lives for the language, though some of us still write in English. A number of us are better, writers already in the old tradition, though expressing something of the life of our time. If I were asked to cite a perfect example of such expression, the natural, almost casual, utterance in sincere, inevitable words of some simple thought or emotion, I should think first of one of the Old Irish poems, like that little poem about the blackbird (*Domfarcai*), and then of a little poem written by

a friend of mine, in an autograph album of all the places
in the world.

Autograph albums I do not like. I have been asked
a few times in my life to write in them, and have always
done so with reluctance. The verses found in them are
rarely poetry. Copies of good poems you will sometimes
meet, but they are then copies in a double sense. They
suffer incongruity. All things are against them—the
handwriting of the copyist, sometimes even of the author—
the little pansies and forget-me-nots hand-painted round
the pages. They suffer nicety and prettiness. But in
one autograph album that I know there is one true poem,
right in its context, right in what I hold to be the essential
qualities of poetry. This album has been on the rounds
for some years, and has accumulated poems by some of
the modern masters, drawings by some of the best artists—
an unusually choice and well-filled album. One feels in
good company when writing in it. At the request of the
owner I sent it some time ago to the Irish writer, Padraig
MacSuibhne, for a contribution. He is not known to be
a poet, yet it is he who wrote the one true poem in the
book. Before I sent it, I looked through it and admired
the gracious little poems, with the good Irish fragrance
in most of them. When I got it back I looked through
it again—page after page of such good verse, in English ;
then on the new page, this Irish protest :

A leabráin, ξαb amaċ ḟá'n ḟaoξal,
Iṡ do ξaċ n-aon dá mbuaileann leaċ
Aiṫṁiṡ cṁuinn ξo maiṁeann Ξaeḋil
Ṫ'ṁéiṡ cleaṡa claon na nξall aṁ ḟad.

(Little book go forth into the world, and unto all that
meet with thee, duly relate that after the wiles of all the
Gall, still live the Gael.)

It is the accent of the best of Dante's *tornate* : it is the
accent of true poetry, simple, sincere, due.

This little poem serves here as an example of what,
to use Arnold's phrase, may be called the note of the new
literature—a note of pride, of self-reliance, almost of
arrogance. The Gaelic revival has given to some of
us a new arrogance. I am a Gael and I know no cause
but of pride in that. Ξaeḋeal mé aξuṡ ní h-eol dom
ξuṡ náiṁ dom é. My race has survived the wiles of
the foreigner here. It has refused to yield even to defeat,
and emerges strong to-day, full of hope and of love, with
new strength in its arms to work its new destiny, with a
new song on its lips and the word of the new language,
which is the ancient language, still calling from age to
age. The adorable delicacy, the shrinking sensibility, the
paralysing diffidence which has its root in charity, the
qualities which make for temporary defeat and yet, being
of their nature joined with the unwavering conviction
of truth and right, for ultimate victory,—these live on.

Now with them, in the same breasts with them, lives this too : its day is come. This arrogance is a sign of energy, of vitality, and so here is good. The Gaelic movement is a revival. Though, through changes of methods and modes of advance, the exhaustion of old methods and the need for new movements, it may seem to-day that the central movement has lost force, it still goes forward. Of a tide of thought, drawn by the inspiration of an ancient cause, there is no ebb. This will have a voice, a literature, to-morrow, the voice of a people new to such a way of speech, the literature of a fresh people. To be a poet one must look with fresh eyes on life ; to produce poets a nation must be fresh. Ireland has already produced a great literature of old : the fragments that remain prove that. But, as we are now, we are a fresh people, fresh to literature. We have begun to produce a literature in English, a foreign tongue. This will not injure or delay the progress of Gaelic literature, which must be the work of other writers. Most of the Anglo-Irish poets— and it is almost all poetry still—have spent in attaining their knowledge and mastery of their craft all the resources of learning and acquirement in them. In the matter of technique—and this is all but supremely necessary in modern poetry—one language only will one poet master. Whether our people go forward in Anglo-Irish literature or not, some of our poets and writers of the

next generation will certainly continue the production
of a new literature in Irish. As I have said, we are
fresh in other senses too—fresh from the natural home
of man, the fields and the country. We have not all
grown up in streets amid the artificialities of civilization,
with traditional memories of brick and plaster. The
influences of nature will be felt by us as by the true poets
of all tongues. Our nature poetry will owe nothing to the
botanical observations of city dwellers ; it will be no sham
pastoral imitation ; it will be natural and spontaneous,
and our own. But above all we are fresh in language,
which the most city-hating English lover of nature cannot
be. We are the children of a race that, through need
or choice, turned from Irish to English. We have now
so well mastered this language of our adoption that we use
it with a freshness and power that the English of these
days rarely have. But now also we have begun to turn
back to the old language, not old to us. The future poets
of the country will probably be the sons and daughters
of a generation that learned Irish as a strange tongue ;
the words and phrases of Irish will have a new wonder
for them ; the figures of speech will have all their first
poetry. Carlyle says of Imagination : " Metaphors are
her stuff ; examine language—what, if you except some
primitive elements, what is it but metaphors, recognised
as such or no longer recognised, still fluid and florid,

or now solid-grown and colourless ? " The metaphors
of Irish will not be colourless to the fresh eyes of the next
generation, though the language be their native idiom.
Perhaps the temporary abandonment of Irish has not been
an unmitigated disaster, now that its revival is assured.
A language that transmits its literature mainly by oral
tradition cannot, if spoken only by thousands, bequeath
as much to posterity as if spoken by millions. The loss
of idiom and of literature is a disaster. But, on the other
hand, the abandonment has broken a tradition of pedantry
and barren conventions ; and sincerity gains thereby.
The *aisling* is now at last dead ; the simple beautiful
folk-songs in which recent Irish literature is richer perhaps than any other, are more likely to serve as models
than the vain word-weaving of the bards. The writers
of the *dán díreach* became at last, to use a mis-translated
phrase, mere " schoolmen of condensed speech," but
their verse at worst had the high virtue of restraint. Their
successors became fluent, eloquent craftsmen of skilful
word-music. The poets of the next age will learn from
the faults of both schools ; they will make restraint a
canon of their art, not a pedantry ; they will know that
the too facile use of the adjective is a vice, and verse-music
a snare. Let us postulate continuity, but continuity in
the true way.

POEMS OF THE IRISH MODE.

OF the Irish Mode which has been the subject of preceding studies, example is the best definition. I am putting together here a number of poems that are unmistakably of this mood. My selection is, of course, nothing in the nature of an anthology ; the poems are printed here to serve as examples and indications, ready at hand, of my meaning   I print no poem that has not good, and indeed evident, warranty. One can easily say of a poem like Mangan's *My Dark Rosaleen* that it is essentially Irish, that it has some indefinable quality not found elsewhere. Frankly I am afraid to rely on those indefinable qualities. If I included *My Dark Rosaleen*, it would be because it is in part a translation of an Irish poem and is full of images and allusions found in Irish poetry. I prefer to take only poems which show one or another of those three influences dealt with in one of my studies : the influence of Irish versification, the influence of the Irish way of speech, the influence of Irish music.

This narrows my choice of course, and endangers my criticism. In spite of all that I say here, it may seem as

if I were denying to some poems, omitted from this
selection, their Irish claim. Some of them are indeed
Irish in all but the marks I look for. *The Little Black
Rose*, by Aubrey de Vere, is as good an example of these
as Mangan's great poem :

"The Little Black Rose shall be red at last ;
    What made it black but the March wind dry,
And the tear of the widow that fell on it fast ?
    It shall redden the hills when June is nigh !

The Silk of the Kine shall rest at last ;
    What drove her forth but the dragon fly ?
In the golden vale she shall feed full fast,
    With her mild gold horn and her slow, dark eye.

The wounded wood-dove lies dead at last !
    The pine long bleeding, it shall not die !
This song is secret. Mine ear it passed
    In a wind o'er the plains at Athenry."

Some poems which lack also these marks are even more
surely Irish, being translations of Gaelic poems, but
translations from syllabic into a form of accentual verse
which has not medial assonances or other graces distinctly
Gaelic. Such is Dr. Sigerson's beautiful *Blackbird of
Daricarn :*

"Sweet thy song, in Dari grove,
    No sweeter song from east to west ;
No music like thy voice of love—
    And thou beneath thy nest !

A strain the softest ever heard,
  No more shall come its like to men.
O Patrick! list the wondrous bird—
  Thou'lt chant thy hymn again.

If thou, as I, but knew the tale
  It sings to all the ancient isle,
Thy tears would rise, and thou wouldst fail
  To mind thy God a while.

In Norroway beyond the wave,
  Its forest glades and streams among,
That bird was found by Fionn the brave,
  And still we hear its song.

'Tis Daricarn yon western wood—
  The Fianna huntsmen loved it best,
And there, on stately oak and good
  Lost Fionn placed its nest.

The tuneful tumult of that bird,
  The belling deer on ferny steep—
This welcome in the dawn he heard,
  These soothed at eve his sleep.

Dear to him the wind-loved heath,
  The whirr of wings, the rustling brake,
Dear the murmuring glens beneath,
  And sob of Droma's lake.

The cry of hounds at early morn,
  The pattering o'er the pebbly creek,
The cuckoo's call, the sounding horn,
  The sweeping eagle's shriek.

> The mountain, not the cell, they sought,
> Great Fionn and the Fianna fleet ;
> Than tinkle of the bells they thought
> The blackbird's song more sweet ! ''

There is still another kind of poem which I cannot use,
a poem which is distinctively of this Irish Mode when
sung to its air or spoken to the rhythm of its air, but capable of being spoken quite naturally in quite another way.
To my ear the lines of this song of Robert Dwyer Joyce's,
which I quote here, have the slow, sweet rhythm of the
lovely air, *An Droighneán Donn* (The Blackthorn), or of
the Irish poem of the name that goes to it ; but I have
heard them riddled off in another way which has shown
me the difference that the association with the music
makes for me :

" By road and by river the wild birds sing,
  O'er mountain and valley the dewy leaves spring,
  The gay flowers are shining, gilt o'er by the sun,
  And fairest of all shines the *Droighnean Donn.*

The rath of the fairy, the ruin hoar,
With white silver splendour it decks them all o'er ;
And down in the valleys, where merry streams run,
How sweet smells the bloom of the *Droighnean Donn!*

Ah ! well I remember the soft spring day,
I sat by my love 'neath its sweet-scented spray ;
The day that she told me her heart I had won,
Beneath the white blossoms of the *Droighnean Donn.*

The streams they were singing their gladsome song,
The soft winds were blowing the wild woods among,
The mountains shone bright in the red setting sun,
And my love in my arms 'neath the *Droighnean Donn*

'Tis my prayer in the morning, my dream at night,
To sit thus again by my heart's dear delight,
With her blue eyes of gladness, her hair like the sun,
And her sweet loving kisses, 'neath the *Droighnean Donn*."

On the other hand I use Mangan's *Vision of Connacht in the Thirteenth Century* as showing the influence on the poet's ear of the rich tolling, in the verse which he studied, of that Gaelic assonance of wider range than any in other languages, broad vowels assonating with other broad and slender with slender, consonants alliterating with others of their class. Read the poem slowly, lingering on the stressed syllables and you will hear the full, rich music.

My examples are largely drawn from the earlier writers. This is, of course, natural ; we trace the river to its springs. I am debarred, moreover, from using here the copyright work of contemporary authors. A few of them are finer poets in this mode and out of it than all but one or two of their predecessors, possibly greater poets than any before them here. Douglas Hyde certainly surpasses all his predecessors as a translator. His influence is probably the most potent felt by the younger poets of the Mode ; the Irish lyrics of Padraic Colum read like other Love-Songs of Connacht omitted from Hyde's book by some extraordinary mishap,—they are so good. The work of George Sigerson, of which I have given above an example, though not a typical one, is unique of its kind. It is of the Irish Mode mainly by virtue of its versification, which, in his translations, is always modelled on his originals. The work of W. B. Yeats may stand with the greatest Anglo-Irish poetry. It may be surpassed by the work of one of his younger contemporaries. His work and theirs would supply me with examples, indeed the best examples, of poetry in this mode influenced by our way of speech and by our music. Professor J. W. Mackail, being asked to make an anthology of Latin Lyric Poetry limited to a hundred pieces, said that it might be plausibly argued that room could be found in such a selection for none but the work of Horace and Catullus. If I had to make an anthology of poems of the Irish Mode limited as is this selection, I could find room only for a small number of pieces by the earlier authors. And that perhaps is the best praise of those authors, paradoxical as it may seem. It is their seed that has flourished in the land.

I deal in one of my studies with some anthologies of Anglo-Irish verse. I wish to close this prosing with a reference for readers to other poets than those already mentioned. The work of Seumas O'Sullivan, Moira O'Neill, Joseph Campbell, Patrick J. McCall, and W. M. Letts is constantly of this mode. Some poems of Æ, Dora Sigerson, J. H. Cousins, Alice Furlong, Hon. Emily Lawless, Thomas Boyd, T. W. Rolleston, and, I think, of Thomas MacDonagh, are of it. The work of some young Irish Poets, of Joseph Plunkett and Peter McBrien, of Susan Mitchell and James Stephens, may well stand to posterity as more Irish, if one may say so, than any of this,—as being most representative of the Irish gifts of fervour and vision which yet may save the world, now being devastated. Their work may so stand in the future ; with such rare exceptions as *Your Fear*, which I print, it does not show the marks I look for, and, as I have already said, I fear suggesting more than I can prove.

N

TRANSLATIONS FROM THE IRISH.

CEANN DUBH DILIS.

Put your head, darling, darling, darling,
    Your darling black head my heart above ;
Oh, mouth of honey, with the thyme for fragrance,
    Who, with heart in breast, could deny you love ?
Oh, many and many a young girl for me is pining,
    Letting her locks of gold to the cold wind free,
For me, the foremost of our gay young fellows ;
    But I'd leave a hundred, pure love, for thee !
Then put your head, darling, darling, darling,
    Your darling black head my heart above ;
Oh, mouth of honey, with the thyme for fragrance,
    Who, with heart in breast, could deny you love ?

SAMUEL FERGUSON.

CASHEL OF MUNSTER.

I'd wed you without herds, without money, or rich
        array,
And I'd wed you on a dewy morning at day-dawn grey ;
My bitter woe it is, love, that we are not far away
In Cashel town, though the bare deal board were our
        marriage bed this day !

Oh, fair maid, remember the green hill-side ;
Remember how I hunted about the valleys wide.
Time now has worn me ; my locks are turned to grey,
The year is scarce and I am poor,—but send me not,
        love, away !

Oh, deem not my blood is of base stain, my girl,
Oh, think not my birth was as the birth of the churl ;
Marry me, and prove me, and say soon you will,
That noble blood is written on my right side still !

My purse holds no red gold, no coin of the silver white,
No herds are mine to drive through the long twilight ;
But the pretty girl that would take me, all bare though I
        be and lone,
Oh, I'd take her with me kindly to the county Tyrone.

Oh, my girl, I can see 'tis in trouble you are,
And, oh, my girl, I see 'tis your people's reproach you
        bear.
—I am a girl in trouble for his sake with whom I fly,
And, oh, may no other maiden know such reproach as I !

                              SAMUEL FERGUSON.

HAVE YOU BEEN AT CARRICK ?

Have you been at Carrick, and saw my true-love there ?
And saw you her features, all beautiful, bright, and
        fair ?
Saw you the most fragrant, flowering, sweet apple-tree ?—
Oh ! saw you my loved one, and pines she in grief like
        me ?

I have been at Carrick, and saw thy own true-love there ;
And saw, too, her features, all beautiful, bright and fair ;
And saw the most fragrant, flowering, sweet apple-tree—
I saw thy loved one—she pines not in grief, like thee !

Five guineas would price every tress of her golden hair—
Then think what a treasure her pillow at night to share,
These tresses thick-clustering and curling around her
    brow—
Oh, Ringlet of Fairness ! I'll drink to thy beauty now !

When seeking to slumber, my bosom is rent with sighs—
I toss on my pillow till morning's blest beams arise ;
No aid, bright Beloved ! can reach me save God above,
For a blood-lake is formed of the light of my eyes with
    love !

Until yellow Autumn shall usher the Paschal day,
And Patrick's gay festival come in its train alway—
Until through my coffin the blossoming boughs shall
    grow,
My love on another I'll never in life bestow !

Lo ! yonder the maiden illustrious, queen-like, high,
With long-flowing tresses adown to her sandal-tie—
Swan, fair as the lily, descended of high degree,
A myriad of welcomes, dear maid of my heart, to thee !

EDWARD WALSH.

THE OUTLAW OF LOCH LENE.

Oh, many a day have I made good ale in the glen,
That came not of stream or malt, like the brewing of
 men.
My bed was the ground ; my roof, the greenwood above,
And the wealth that I sought one far kind glance from
 my love.

Alas ! on that night when the horses I drove from the
 field,
That I was not near from terror my angel to shield.
She stretched forth her arms,—her mantle she flung
 to the wind,
And swam o'er Loch Lene, her outlawed lover to find.

Oh, would that a freezing sleet-wing'd tempest did sweep,
And I and my love were alone, far off on the deep ;
I'd ask not a ship, or a bark, or pinnace, to save,—
With her hand round my waist, I'd fear not the wind or
 the wave.

'Tis down by the lake where the wild-tree fringes its
 sides,
The maid of my heart, my fair one of Heaven resides ;—
I think as at eve she wanders its mazes along,
The birds go to sleep by the sweet wild twist of her song.

J. J. CALLANAN.

PASTHEEN FINN

Oh, my fair Pastheen is my heart's delight ;
Her gay heart laughs in her blue eye bright ;
Like the apple blossom her bosom white,
And her neck like the swan's on a March morn bright !
    Then, Oro, come with me ! come with me ! come
      with me !
    Oro, come with me ! brown girl, sweet !
    And, oh ! I would go through snow and sleet
    If you would come with me, brown girl, sweet !

Love of my heart, my fair Pastheen !
Her cheeks are as red as the rose's sheen,
But my lips have tasted no more, I ween,
Than the glass I drank to the health of my queen !
    Then, Oro, come with me ! come with me ! come
      with me !
    Oro, come with me ! brown girl, sweet !
    And, oh ! I would go through snow and sleet
    If you would come with me, brown girl, sweet !

Were I in the town, where's mirth and glee,
Or 'twixt two barrels of barley bree,
With my fair Pastheen upon my knee,
'Tis I would drink to her pleasantly !
    Then, Oro, come with me ! come with me ! come
      with me !
    Oro, come with me ! brown girl, sweet !
    And, oh ! I would go through snow and sleet
    If you would come with me, brown girl, sweet !

Nine nights I lay in longing and pain,
Betwixt two bushes, beneath the rain,
Thinking to see you, love, once again ;
But whistle and call were all in vain !
 Then, Oro, come with me ! come with me ! come
  with me !
 Oro, come with me ! brown girl, sweet !
 And, oh ! I would go through snow and sleet
 If you would come with me, brown girl, sweet !

I'll leave my people, both friend and foe ;
From all the girls in the world I'll go ;
But from you, sweetheart, oh, never ! oh, no !
Till I lie in the coffin, stretched cold and low !
 Then, Oro, come with me ! come with me ! come
  with me !
 Oro, come with me ! brown girl, sweet !
 And, oh ! I would go through snow and sleet
 If you would come with me, brown girl, sweet.

SAMUEL FERGUSON.

THE COOLUN.

Oh, had you seen the Coolun,
 Walking down by the cuckoo's street,
With the dew of the meadow shining
 On her milk-white twinkling feet.
My love she is, and my *cailin óg*
 And she dwells in Bal'nagar ;
And she bears the palm of beauty bright
 From the fairest that in Erin are.

In Bal'nagar is the Coolun,
   Like the berry on the bough her cheek ;
Bright beauty dwells for ever
   On her fair neck and ringlets sleek ;
Oh, sweeter is her mouth's soft music
   Than the lark or thrush at dawn,
Or the blackbird in the greenwood singing
   Farewell to the setting sun.

Rise up, my boy ! make ready
   My horse, for I forth would ride,
To follow the modest damsel,
   Where she walks on the green hill-side :
For ever since our youth were we plighted,
   In faith, troth, and wedlock true—
Oh, she's sweeter to me nine times over
   Than organ or cuckoo !

For ever since my childhood
   I loved the fair and darling child ;
But our people came between us,
   And with lucre our pure love defiled :
Oh, my woe it is, and my bitter pain,
   And I weep it night and day,
That the *cailin bán* of my early love
   Is torn from my heart away.

Sweetheart and faithful treasure,
   Be constant still, and true ;
Nor for want of herds and houses
   Leave one who would ne'er leave you.

I'll pledge you the blessed Bible,
  Without and eke within,
That the faithful God will provide for us,
  Without thanks to kith or kin.

Oh, love, do you remember
  When we lay all night alone,
Beneath the ash in the winter storm,
  When the oak wood round did groan ?
No shelter then from the blast had we,
  The bitter blast or sleet,
But your gown to wrap about our heads,
  And my coat round our feet.

SAMUEL FERGUSON.

PULSE OF MY HEART.

Before the sun rose at yester-dawn,
I met a fair maid adown the lawn :
    The berry and snow
    To her cheek gave its glow,
And her bosom was fair as the sailing swan—
Then, pulse of my heart ! what gloom is thine ?

Her beautiful voice more hearts hath won
Than Orpheus' lyre of old had done ;
    Her ripe eyes of blue
    Were crystals of dew,
On the grass of the lawn before the sun—
And, pulse of my heart ! what gloom is thine ?

EDWARD WALSH.

ISN'T IT PLEASANT FOR THE LITTLE BIRDS.

Isn't it pleasant for the little birds
   That rise up above,
And be nestling together
   On the one branch, in love ?
Not so with myself
   And the darling of my heart—
Every day rises upon us
   Far, far apart.

She is whiter than the lily,
   Than beauty more fine.
She is sweeter than the violin,
   More radiant than the sunshine.
But her grace and her nobleness
   Are beyond all that again—
And, O God Who art in Heaven,
   Free me from pain !

PEARL OF THE WHITE BREAST.

There's a colleen fair as May,
For a year and for a day
I've sought by every way—Her heart to gain.
There's no art of tongue or eye,
Fond youths with maidens try,
But I've tried with ceaseless sigh—Yet tried in vain.
If to France or far-off Spain,
She'd cross the watery main,
To see her face again—The sea I'd brave.

And if 'tis Heaven's decree,
That mine she may not be,
May the Son of Mary me—In mercy save !

Oh, thou blooming milk-white dove,
To whom I've given true love,
Do not ever thus reprove—My constancy.
There are maidens would be mine,
With wealth in hand and kine,
If my heart would but incline—To turn from thee,
But a kiss, with welcome bland,
And a touch of thy dear hand,
Are all that I demand,—Wouldst thou not spurn ;
For if not mine, dear girl,
Oh, Snowy-breasted Pearl !
May I never from the Fair—With life return !

GEORGE PETRIE.

THE COUNTY OF MAYO.

(BY THOMAS FLAVELL.)

On the deck of Patrick Lynch's boat I sat in woful
    plight,
Through my sighing all the weary day, and weeping
    all the night ;
Were it not that full of sorrow from my people forth
    I go,
By the blessèd sun ! 'tis royally I'd sing thy praise,
    Mayo !

When I dwelt at home in plenty, and my gold did much
    abound,
In the company of fair young maids the Spanish ale went
    round—
'Tis a bitter change from those gay days that now I'm
    forced to go,
And must leave my bones in Santa Cruz, far from my
    own Mayo.

They are altered girls in Irrul now ; 'tis proud they're
    grown and high,
With their hair-bags and their top-knots, for I pass their
    buckles by—
But it's little now I heed their airs, for God will have
    it so,
That I must depart for foreign lands, and leave my sweet
    Mayo.

'Tis my grief that Patrick Loughlin is not Earl of Irrul
    still,
And that Brian Duff no longer rules as Lord upon the
    hill :
And that Colonel Hugh MacGrady should be lying dead
    and low,
And I sailing, sailing swiftly from the county of Mayo.

                                GEORGE FOX.

THE FAIR HILLS OF IRELAND.

A plenteous place is Ireland for hospitable cheer,
    Uileacan dubh O !
Where the wholesome fruit is bursting from the yellow
    barley ear ;
        Uileacan dubh O !
There is honey in the trees where her misty vales
    expand,
And her forest paths in summer are by falling waters
    fanned ;
There is dew at high noontide there, and springs i' the
    yellow sand,
    On the fair hills of holy Ireland.

Curled he is and ringleted, and plaited to the knee,
        Uileacan dubh O !
Each captain who comes sailing across the Irish sea ;
        Uileacan dubh O !
And I will make my journey, if life and health but
    stand,
Unto that pleasant country, that fresh and fragrant
    strand,
And leave your boasted braveries, your wealth and high
    command,
    For the fair hills of holy Ireland.

Large and profitable are the stacks upon the ground ;
        Uileacan dubh O !
The butter and the cream do wondrously abound ;
        Uileacan dubh O !

The cresses on the water and the sorrels are at hand,
And the cuckoo's calling daily his note of music bland,
And the bold thrush sings so bravely his song i' the forests
     grand,
  On the fair hills of holy Ireland.

SAMUEL FERGUSON.

LAMENTATION OF MAC LIAG FOR KINCORA.

Oh, where, Kincora ! is Brian the Great ?
And where is the beauty that once was thine ?
Oh, where are the princes and nobles that sate
At the feast in thy halls, and drank the red wine ?
       Where, O Kincora ?

Oh, where, Kincora ! are thy valorous lords ?
Oh, whither, thou Hospitable ! are they gone ?
Oh, where are the Dalcassians of the Golden Swords ?
And where are the warriors Brian led on ?
       Where, O Kincora ?

And where is Murrough, the descendant of kings—
The defeater of a hundred—the daringly brave—
Who set but slight store by jewels and rings—
Who swam down the torrent and laughed at its wave ?
       Where, O Kincora ?

And where is Donogh, King Brian's worthy son ?
And where is Conaing, the Beautiful Chief ?
And Kian, and Corc ? Alas ! they are gone—
They have left me this night alone with my grief !
       Left me, Kincora !

And where are the chiefs with whom Brian went forth,
The ne'er-vanquished son of Evin the Brave,
The great King of Onaght, renowned for his worth,
And the hosts of Baskinn, from the western wave ?
        Where, O Kincora ?

Oh, where is Duvlann of the Swift-footed Steeds ?
And where is Kian, who was son of Molloy ?
And where is King Lonergan, the fame of whose deeds
In the red battle-field no time can destroy ?
        Where, O Kincora ?

And where is that youth of majestic height,
The faith-keeping Prince of the Scots ?—Even he,
As wide as his fame was, as great as was his might,
Was tributary, O Kincora, to thee !
        Thee, O Kincora !

They are gone, those heroes of royal birth,
Who plundered no churches, and broke no trust,
'Tis weary for me to be living on earth
When they, O Kincora, lie low in the dust !
        Low, O Kincora !

Oh, never again will Princes appear,
To rival the Dalcassians of the Cleaving Swords !
I can never dream of meeting afar or anear,
In the east or the west, such heroes and lords !
        Never, Kincora !

Oh, dear are the images my memory calls up
Of Brian Boru !—how he never would miss
To give me at the banquet the first bright cup !
Ah ! why did he heap on me honour like this ?
          Why, O Kincora ?

I am MacLiag, and my home is on the Lake ;
Thither often, to that palace whose beauty is fled,
Came Brian to ask me, and I went for his sake.
Oh, my grief ! that I should live, and Brian be dead !
          Dead, O Kincora !

                    JAMES CLARENCE MANGAN.

———

A FAREWELL TO PATRICK SARSFIELD,
EARL OF LUCAN.

Farewell, O Patrick Sarsfield, may luck be on your path !
    Your camp is broken up, your work is marred for years ;
But you go to kindle into flame the King of France's wrath,
    Though you leave sick Eire in tears—
          Och, ochone !

May the white sun and moon rain glory on your head,
    All hero as you are, and holy man of God !
To you the Saxons owe a many an hour of dread
    In the land you have often trod—
          Och, ochone !

The Son of Mary guard you, and bless you to the end !
'Tis altered is the time when your legions were astir,
When at Cullen you were hailed as conqueror and friend,
    And you crossed Narrow-water, near Birr—
            Och, ochone !

I'll journey to the north, over mount, moor, and wave ;
'Twas there I first beheld drawn up, in file and line,
The brilliant Irish hosts ; they were bravest of the brave,
    But, alas, they scorned to combine—
            Och, ochone !

I saw the royal Boyne when his billows flashed with blood ;
I fought at Graine Og, when a thousand horsemen fell ;
On the dark empurpled plain of Aughrim, too, I stood,
    On the plain by Tubberdonny's well—
            Och, ochone !

To the heroes of Limerick, the City of the Fights,
    Be my best blessing borne on the wings of the air ;
We had card-playing there o'er our camp fires at night,
    And the Word of Life, too, and prayer—
            Och, ochone !

But for you, Londonderry, may plague smite and slay
    Your people ! May ruin desolate you stone by stone !
Through you there's many a gallant youth lies coffinless
    to-day
With the winds for mourners alone—
            Och, ochone !

o

I clomb the high hill on a fair summer noon,
  And saw the Saxons muster, clad in armour blinding
    bright :
Oh, rage withheld my hand, or gunsman and dragoon
  Should have supped with Satan that night !—
          Och, ochone !

How many a noble soldier, how many a cavalier,
  Careered along this road, seven fleeting weeks ago,
With silver-hilted sword, with matchlock and with spear,
  Who now, *mo bhrón !* lieth low—
          Och, ochone !

All hail to thee, Beinn Eidir ! but ah, on thy brow
  I see a limping soldier, who battled and who bled
Last year in the cause of the Stuart, though now
  The worthy is begging his bread—
          Och, ochone !

And Diarmid ! oh, Diarmid ! he perished in the strife ;
  His head it was spiked upon a halberd high ;
His colours they were trampled : he had no chance of life
  If the Lord God Himself stood by !—
          Och, ochone !

But most, oh, my woe ! I lament and lament
  For the ten valiant heroes who dwelt nigh the Nore,
And my three blessed brothers ; they left me and went
  To the wars, and returned no more—
          Och, ochone !

On the bridge of the Boyne was our first overthrow ;
  By Slaney the next, for we battled without rest ;
The third was at Aughrim. O Eire ! thy woe
  Is a sword in my bleeding breast—
                Och, ochone !

Oh, the roof above our heads, it was barbarously fired,
  While the black Orange guns blazed and bellowed
    around !
And as volley followed volley, Colonel Mitchel inquired
  Whether Lucan still stood his ground ?—
                Och, ochone !

But O'Kelly still remains, to defy and to toil,
  He has memories that hell won't permit him to forget,
And a sword that will make the blue blood flow like oil
  Upon many an Aughrim yet !—
                Och, ochone !

And I never shall believe that my fatherland can fall
  With the Burkes, and the Dukes, and the son of Royal
    James,
And Talbot, the captain, and Sarsfield above all,
  The beloved of damsels and dames—
                Och, ochone !

                   JAMES CLARENCE MANGAN.

KATHALEEN NY-HOULAHAN.

(BY WILLIAM HEFFERNAN.)

Long they pine in weary woe, the nobles of our land,
Long they wander to and fro, proscribed, alas! and
    banned ;
Feastless, houseless, altarless, they bear the exile's brand ;
    But their hope is in the coming-to of Kathaleen
    Ny-Houlahan !

Think her not a ghastly hag, too hideous to be seen,
Call her not unseemly names, our matchless Kathaleen ;
Young she is, and fair she is, and would be crowned
    a queen,
    Were the king's son at home here with Kathaleen
    Ny-Houlahan !

Sweet and mild would look her face, oh! none so sweet
    and mild,
Could she crush the foes by whom her beauty is reviled ;
Woollen plaids would grace herself, and robes of silk
    her child,
    If the king's son were living here with Kathaleen
    Ny-Houlahan !

Sore disgrace it is to see the Arbitress of thrones,
Vassal to a Saxoneen of cold and sapless bones !
Bitter anguish wrings our souls—with heavy sighs and
    groans
    We wait the young Deliverer of Kathaleen
    Ny-Houlahan !

Let us pray to Him who holds life's issues in His hands—
Him who formed the mighty globe, with all its thousand
    lands,
Girdling them with seas and mountains, rivers deep, and
    strands,
    To cast a look of pity upon Kathaleen Ny-Houlahan !

He who over sands and waves led Israel along—
He who fed, with heavenly bread, that chosen tribe and
    throng—
He who stood by Moses, when his foes were fierce and
    strong—
    May He show forth His might in saving Kathaleen
    Ny-Houlahan !

JAMES CLARENCE MANGAN.

EAMONN AN CHNUIC.

—Who is that out there still
With voice sharp and shrill,
Beating my door and calling ?
—I am Ned of the Hill,
Wet, weary and chill,
The mountains and glens long walking.

—O my dear love and true !
What could I do for you
But under my mantle draw you ?
For the bullets like hail
Fall thick on your trail,
And together we both may be slaughtered.

—Long lonely I go,
Under frost, under snow,
Hunted through hill and through hollow.
No comrade I know :
No furrow I sow :
My team stands unyoked in the fallow :

No friend will give ear
Or harbour me here,—
'Tis that makes the weight of my sorrow !
So my journey must be
To the east o'er the sea
Where no kindred will find me or follow !

DRUIMFHIONN DONN DILIS.

—O Druimfhionn Donn Dilis !
O Silk of the Kine !
Where goest thou for sleeping ?
What pastures are thine ?
—In the woods with my gilly
Always I must keep,
And 'tis that now that leaves me
Forsaken to weep.

Land, homestead, wines, music :
I am reft of them all !
Chief and bard that once wooed me
Are gone from my call !

And cold water to soothe me
I sup with my tears,
While the foe that pursues me
Has drinking that cheers.

—Through the mist of the glensides
And hills I'll return :
Like a brogue beyond mending
The Sasanach I'll spurn :
If in battle's contention
I have sight of the crown,
I'll befriend thee and defend thee,
My young Druimfhionn Donn !

THE YELLOW BITTERN.

(By Cathal Buidhe Mac Giolla Ghunna.)

The yellow bittern that never broke out
    In a drinking bout, might as well have drunk ;
His bones are thrown on a naked stone
    Where he lived alone like a hermit monk.
O yellow bittern ! I pity your lot,
    Though they say that a sot like myself is curst—
I was sober a while, but I'll drink and be wise
    For fear I should die in the end of thirst.

It's not for the common birds that I'd mourn,
    The black-bird, the corn-crake or the crane,
But for the bittern that's shy and apart
    And drinks in the marsh from the lone bog-drain.

Oh ! if I had known you were near your death,
   While my breath held out I'd have run to you,
Till a splash from the Lake of the Son of the Bird
   Your soul would have stirred and waked anew.

My darling told me to drink no more
   Or my life would be o'er in a little short while ;
But I told her 'tis drink gives me health and strength
   And will lengthen my road by many a mile.
You see how the bird of the long smooth neck
   Could get his death from the thirst at last—
Come, son of my soul, and drain your cup,
   You'll get no sup when your life is past.

In a wintering island by Constantine's halls
   A bittern calls from a wineless place,
And tells me that hither he cannot come
   Till the summer is here and the sunny days.
When he crosses the stream there and wings o'er the sea
   Then a fear comes to me he may fail in his flight—
Well, the milk and the ale are drunk every drop,
   And a dram won't stop our thirst this night.

———

THE SONG OF GLADNESS.

(By William Heffernan.)

It was on a balmy evening, as June was departing fast,
That alone, and meditating in grief on the times a-past,
   I wandered through the gloomsome shades
      Of bosky Aherlow,
   A wilderness of glens and glades,

When suddenly a thrilling strain of song
    Broke forth upon the air in one incessant flow ;
    Sweeter it seemed to me (both voice and word)
    Than harmony of the harp, or carol of the bird,
For it foretold fair Freedom's triumph, and the doom of
    Wrong.

The celestial hymns and anthems, that far o'er the sound-
    ing sea
Come to Erin from the temples of bright-bosomed
    Italy ;
    The music which from hill and rath
    The playful fairy race
    Pour on the wandering warrior's path,
Bewildering him with wonder and delight,
    Or the cuckoo's full note from some green sunless
    place,
    Some sunken thicket in a stilly wood,
    Had less than that rich melody made mine Irish
    blood
Bound in its veins for ecstasy, or given my soul new
    might !

And while as I stood I listened, behold, thousand swarm
    of bees,
All arrayed in gay gold armour, shone red through the
    dusky trees ;
    I felt a boding in my soul,
    A truthful boding, too,
    That Erin's days of gloom and dole

Will soon be but remembered as a dream,
　　And the olden glory show eclipsèd by the new.
　　Where will the Usurper then be ?　Banished far !
　　Where his vile hireling henchmen ?　Slaughtered all
　　　　in war !
For blood shall rill down every hill, and blacken every
　　stream.

I am Heffernan of Shronehill :　my　land ˙ mourns in
　　thraldom long ;
And I see but one sad sight here, the weak trampled by
　　the strong,
　　Yet if to-morrow underneath
　　A burial-stone I lay,
Clasped in the skeleton arms of death.
And if a pilgrim wind again should waft
　　Over my noteless grave the song I heard to-day,
　　I would spring up revivified, reborn,
　　A living soul again, as on my birthday morn,
Ay !　even though coffined, over-earthed, tombed-in, and
　　epitaphed !

JAMES CLARENCE MANGAN.

BALLADS AND STREET SONGS.

SHULE AROON.

A BRIGADE BALLAD.

I wish I were on yonder hill,
'Tis there I'd sit and cry my fill
Till every tear would turn a mill,
Is go dtéidh tú, a mhuirnín, slán!

> *Siubhail, siubhail, siubhail, a rúin!*
> *Siubhail go socair, agus siubhail go ciuin,*
> *Siubhail go dti an dorus agus eulaigh liom,*
> *Is go dtéidh tú, a mhuirnín, slán!*

I'll sell my rock, I'll sell my reel,
I'll sell my only spinning-wheel,
To buy for my love a sword of steel,
Is go dtéidh tú, a mhuirnín, slán!

I'll dye my petticoats, I'll dye them red,
And round the world I'll beg my bread,
Until my parents will wish me dead,
Is go dtéidh tú, a mhuirnín, slán!

I wish, I wish, I wish in vain,
I wish I had my heart again,
And vainly think I'd not complain,
Is go dtéidh tú, a mhuirnin, slán!

But now my love has gone to France,
To try his fortune to advance ;
If he e'er come back 'tis but a chance,
Is go dtéidh tú, a mhuirnin, slán!

ANONYMOUS.

THE CROPPY BOY

It was very early in the spring,
The birds did whistle and sweetly sing,
Changing their notes from tree to tree,
And the song they sang was Old Ireland free.

It was early in the night,
The yeoman cavalry gave me a fright ;
The yeoman cavalry was my downfall.
And taken was I by Lord Cornwall.

'Twas in the guard-house where I was laid
And in a parlour where I was tried ;
My sentence passed and my courage low
When to Dungannon I was forced to go.

As I was passing by my father's door,
My brother William stood at the door ;
My aged father stood at the door,
And my tender mother her hair she tore.

As I was walking up Wexford Street
My own first cousin I chanced to meet :
My own first cousin did me betray,
And for one bare guinea swore my life away.

My sister Mary heard the express,
She ran upstairs in her mourning-dress—
Five hundred guineas I will lay down,
To see my brother through Wexford Town.

As I was walking up Wexford Hill,
Who could blame me to cry my fill ?
I looked behind and I looked before,
But my tender mother I shall ne'er see more.

As I was mounted on the platform high,
My aged father was standing by ;
My aged father did me deny,
And the name he gave me was the Croppy Boy.

It was in Dungannon this young man died,
And in Dungannon his body lies ;
And you good Christians that do pass by
Just drop a tear for the Croppy Boy.

ANONYMOUS.

THE STREAMS OF BUNCLODY.

Oh, was I at the moss-house where the birds do increase,
At the foot of Mount Leinster or some silent place
Near the streams of Bunclody, where all pleasures do
       meet,
And all I'd require is one kiss from you, sweet.

If I was in Bunclody I would think myself at home,
'Tis there I would have a sweetheart, but here I have
none.
Drinking strong liquor in the height of my cheer—
Here's a health to Bunclody and the lass I love dear.

The cuckoo is a pretty bird, it sings as it flies,
It brings us good tidings and tells us no lies,
It sucks the young bird's eggs to make its voice clear,
And it never cries cuckoo till the summer is near.

If I was a clerk and could write a good hand,
I would write to my true love that she might understand,
I am a young fellow that is wounded in love,
That lived by Bunclody, but now must remove.

If I was a lark and had wings, I then could fly,
I would go to yon arbour where my love she doth lie,
I'd proceed to yon arbour where my love does lie,
And on her fond bosom contented I would die.

The reason my love slights me, as you may understand,
Because she has a freehold, and I have no land,
She has a great store of riches and a large sum of gold,
And everything fitting a house to uphold.

So adieu, my dear father, adieu, my dear mother,
Farewell to my sister, farewell to my brother ;
I'm going to America, my fortune for to try ;
When I think upon Bunclody, I'm ready for to die !

ANONYMOUS.

THE GROVES OF BLARNEY.

The groves of Blarney they look so charming,
Down by the purling of sweet, silent streams,
Being banked with posies that spontaneous grow there,
Planted in order by the sweet rock close.
'Tis there's the daisy and the sweet carnation,
The blooming pink and the rose so fair,
The daffadowndilly, likewise the lily,
All flowers that scent the sweet, fragrant air.

'Tis Lady Jeffers that owns this station ;
Like Alexander, or Queen Helen fair,
There's no commander in all the nation,
For emulation, can with her compare.
Such walls surround her, that no nine-pounder
Could dare to plunder her place of strength ;
But Oliver Cromwell her he did pommel,
And made a breach in her battlement.

There's gravel walks there for speculation
And conversation in sweet solitude.
'Tis there the lover may hear the dove, or
The gentle plover in the afternoon ;
And if a lady would be so engaging
As to walk alone in those shady bowers,
'Tis there the courtier he may transport her
Into some fort, or all under ground.

For 'tis there's a cave where no daylight enters,
But cats and badgers are for ever bred ;
Being mossed by nature, that makes it sweeter
Than a coach-and-six or a feather bed.

'Tis there the lake is, well stored with perches,
And comely eels in the verdant mud ;
Besides the leeches, and groves of beeches,
Standing in order for to guard the flood.

There's statues gracing this noble place in—
All heathen gods and nymphs so fair ;
Bold Neptune, Plutarch, and Nicodemus,
All standing naked in the open air !
So now to finish this brave narration,
Which my poor genii could not entwine ;
But were I Homer, or Nebuchadnezzar,
'Tis in every feature I would make it shine.

                                    R. A. MILLIKEN.

ORIGINAL POEMS.

AT THE MID HOUR OF NIGHT.

At the mid hour of night, when stars are weeping, I fly
To the lone vale we loved, when life shone warm in thine
    eye ;
  And I think oft, if spirits can steal from the regions
    of air,
  To revisit past scenes of delight, thou wilt come to
    me there,
And tell me our love is remembered, even in the sky.

Then I sing the wild song it once was rapture to hear
When our voices, commingling, breathed like one on
    the ear ;
  And as Echo far off through the vale my sad orison
    rolls,
  I think, O my love ! 'tis thy voice from the Kingdom
    of Souls,
Faintly answering still the notes that once were so dear.

THOMAS MOORE.

THE STARLING LAKE.

My sorrow that I am not by the little dún
By the lake of the starlings at Rosses under the hill,
And the larks there, singing over the fields of dew,
Or evening there and the sedges still.
For plain I see now the length of the yellow sand,
And Lissadell far off and its leafy ways,
And the holy mountain whose mighty heart
Gathers into it all the coloured days.

My sorrow that I am not by the little dún
By the lake of the starlings at evening when all is still,
And still in whispering sedges the herons stand.
'Tis there I would nestle at rest till the quivering moon
Uprose in the golden quiet over the hill.

SEUMAS O'SULLIVAN.

THE IRISH PEASANT TO HIS MISTRESS

Through grief and through danger thy smile hath cheered
          my way,
Till hope seemed to bud from each thorn that round me
          lay ;
The darker our fortune, the brighter our pure love burned,
Till shame into glory, till fear into zeal was turned.
Oh ! slave that I was, in thy arms my spirit felt free,
And blessed e'en the sorrows that made me more dear to
          thee.

Thy rival was honoured, while thou wert wronged and
    scorned ;
Thy crown was of briars, while gold her brows adorned ;
She wooed me to temples, while thou layst hid in caves ;
Her friends were all masters, while thine, alas ! were
    slaves ;
Yet cold in the earth at thy feet I'd rather be
Than wed what I loved not, or turn one thought from
    thee.

They slander thee sorely who say thy vows are frail ;
Hadst thou been a false one, thy cheek had looked less
    pale ;
They say, too, so long thou hast worn those lingering
    chains,
That deep in thy heart they have printed their servile
    stains,—
Oh ! do not believe them, no chain could that soul
    subdue :
Where shineth thy spirit, there liberty shineth too.

THOMAS MOORE.

A VISION OF CONNAUGHT IN THE THIRTEENTH CENTURY.

I walked entranced
    Through a land of Morn :
The sun, with wondrous excess of light,
    Shone down and glanced
      Over seas of corn
And lustrous gardens aleft and right.

Even in the clime
Of resplendent Spain,
Beams no such sun upon such a land ;
But it was the time,
'Twas in the reign,
Of Cahal Mór of the Wine-red Hand.

Anon stood nigh
By my side a man
Of princely aspect and port sublime
Him queried I—
" O, my Lord and Khan,
What clime is this, and what golden time ? "
When he—"The clime
Is a clime to praise,
The clime is Erin's, the green and bland ;
And it is the time,
These be the days,
Of Cahal Mór of the Wine-red Hand ! "

Then saw I thrones
And circling fires,
And a Dome rose near me, as by a spell,
Whence flowed the tones
Of silver lyres,
And many voices in wreathèd swell ;
And their thrilling chime
Fell on mine ears
As the heavenly hymn of an angel-band—
" It is now the time
These be the years,
Of Cahal Mór of the Wine-red Hand ¡ "

I sought the hall,
    And, behold !—a change
From light to darkness, from joy to woe !
    King, nobles, all,
        Looked aghast and strange ;
The minstrel-group sate in dumbest show !
    Had some great crime
        Wrought this dread amaze,
This terror ?   None seemed to understand
    'Twas then the time,
        We were in the days,
Of Cahal Mór of the Wine-red Hand.

    I again walked forth ;
        But lo ! the sky
Showed fleckt with blood, and an alien sun
    Glared from the north,
        And there stood on high,
Amid his shorn beams, a skeleton !
    It was by the stream
        Of the castled Maine,
One Autumn eve, in the Teuton's land,
    That I dreamed this dream
        Of the time and reign
Of Cahal Mór of the Wine-red Hand !

                        JAMES CLARENCE MANGAN

YOUR FEAR.

I try to blame
When from your eyes the battle-flame
Leaps—when cleaves my speech the spear
For fear lest I should speak your name.

Your name, that's known
But to your heart, you fear has flown
To mine—You've heard not any bird,
No wings have stirred save yours alone.

Alone your wings
Have fluttered : half-forgotten things
Come crowding home into your heart,
Filling your heart with other Springs :

Springs when you've sung
Your secret name with happy tongue
Loudly and innocent as the flowers
Through hours of laughter proudly young.

Young is the year
And other wings are waking : near
Your heart my name is knocking loud—
Ah, be not proud ! You need not fear.

Fearing lest I
Should wrest your secret from on high
You will not listen to my name—
I cannot blame you though I try.

JOSEPH PLUNKETT.

THE FAIRY THORN.

AN ULSTER BALLAD.

" Get up, our Anna dear, from the weary spinning-wheel ;
 For your father's on the hill, and your mother is asleep :
Come up above the crags, and we'll dance a Highland
  reel
 Around the Fairy Thorn on the steep."

At Anna Grace's door 'twas thus the maidens cried,
 Three merry maidens fair in kirtles of the green ;
And Anna laid the rock and the weary wheel aside,
 The fairest of the four, I ween.

They're glancing through the glimmer of the quiet eve,
 Away in milky wavings of neck and ankle bare ;
The heavy-sliding stream in its sleepy song they leave,
 And the crags in the ghostly air.

And linking hand-in-hand, and singing as they go,
 The maids along the hill-side have ta'en their fearless
  way,
Till they come to where the rowan trees in lonely beauty
  grow
 Beside the Fairy Hawthorn grey.

The Hawthorn stands between the ashes tall and slim,
 Like matron with her twin grand-daughters at her
  knee ;
The rowan berries cluster o'er her low head grey and dim
 In ruddy kisses sweet to see.

The merry maidens four have ranged them in a row,
    Between each lovely couple a stately rowan stem,
And away in mazes wavy, like skimming birds they go,
    Oh, never carolled bird like them !

But solemn is the silence of the silvery haze
    That drinks away their voices in echoless repose,
And dreamily the evening has stilled the haunted braes,
    And dreamier the gloaming grows.

And sinking one by one, like lark-notes from the sky,
    When the falcon's shadow saileth across the open shaw,
Are hushed the maidens' voices, as cowering down they
        lie
    In the flutter of their sudden awe.

For, from the air above and the grassy ground beneath,
    And from the mountain-ashes and the old Whitethorn
        between,
A Power of faint enchantment doth through their beings
        breathe,
    And they sink down together on the green.

They sink together silent, and stealing side to side,
    They fling their lovely arms o'er their drooping necks
        so fair,
Then vainly strive again their naked arms to hide,
    For their shrinking necks again are bare.

Thus clasped and prostrate all, with their heads together
        bowed,
    Soft o'er their bosoms' beating—the only human
        sound—

They hear the silky footsteps of the silent fairy crowd,
  Like a river in the air gliding round

Nor scream can any raise, nor prayer can any say,
  But wild, wild the terror of the speechless three—
For they feel fair Anna Grace drawn silently away,
  By whom they dare not look to see

They feel their tresses twine with her parting locks of
    gold,
  And the curls elastic falling, as her head withdraws ;
They feel her sliding arms from their trancèd arms unfold,
  But they dare not look to see the cause ;

For heavy on their senses the faint enchantment lies
  Through all that night of anguish and perilous amaze ;
And neither fear nor wonder can ope their quivering eyes,
  Or their limbs from the cold ground raise ;

Till out of night the earth has rolled her dewy side,
  With every haunted mountain and streamy vale below ;
When, as the mist dissolves in the yellow morning tide,
  The maidens' trance dissolveth so

Then fly the ghastly three as swiftly as they may,
  And tell their tale of sorrow to anxious friends in vain—
They pined away and died within the year and day,
  And ne'er was Anna Grace seen again.

SAMUEL FERGUSON.

THE LARK IN THE CLEAR AIR.

Dear thoughts are in my mind,
And my soul soars enchanted,
As I hear the sweet lark sing,
In the clear air of the day.
For a tender beaming smile,
To my hope has been granted,
And to-morrow she shall hear,
All my fond heart would say.

I shall tell her all my love,
All my soul's adoration,
And I think she will hear me,
And will not say me nay.
It is this that gives my soul
All its joyous elation,
As I hear the sweet lark sing,
In the clear air of the day.

SAMUEL FERGUSON.

MAY DAY.

I wish I were to-day on the hill behind the wood,—
My eyes on the brown bog there and the Shannon river,—
Behind the wood at home, a quickened solitude
When the winds from Slieve Bloom set the branches
          there a-quiver.

The winds are there now and the green of May
On every feathery tree-bough, tender on every hedge :
Over the bog-fields there larks carol to-day,
And a cuckoo is mocking them out of the woodland's
    edge.

Here a country warmth is quiet on the rocks
That alone make never a change when the May is duly
    come ;
Here sings no lark, and to-day no cuckoo mocks :
Over the wide hill a hawk floats, and the leaves are dumb.

———

THE TRIAD OF THINGS NOT DECREED.

Happy the stark bare wood on the hill of Bree !
To its grey branch, green of the May : song after sigh :
Laughter of wings where the wind went with a cry
My sorrow ! Song after sigh comes not to me

Happy the dry wide pastures by Ahenree !
To them, in the speckled twilight, dew after drouth :
White clover, a fragrance in the dumb beast's mouth.
My sorrow ! Dew after drouth comes not to me.

Happy Oilean Acla in the ample sea !
To its yellow shore, long-billowed flood after ebb :
Flash of the fish, silver in the sloak weeds' web.
My sorrow ! Flood after ebb comes not to me.

ALICE FURLONG.

NOTES.

Page 2. *The Triads of Ireland* : A collection of wise sayings made at the end of the ninth century. Examples : Three candles that illume every darkness : truth, nature, knowledge. Three rude ones of the world : a youngster mocking an old man, a robust person mocking an invalid, a wise man mocking a fool. *The Triads* have been edited and translated by Kuno Meyer in the Todd Lecture Series of the Royal Irish Academy, vol. xiii. (Hodges, Figgis & Co., Dublin.)

Page 6. *La Belle Dame Sans Merci*. In the *Life and Letters of John Keats*, Lord Houghton tells how the sheets on which Keats had written his *Ode to a Nightingale* were thrust away by the author, " as waste paper, behind some books," and the difficulty that his friend Brown had in putting together and arranging the stanzas of the ode. Among " other poems as literally ' fugitive,' rescued in much the same way," he gives " a ballad of much grace and tenderness, and expressive of the feelings that were then growing fast within him." It is *La Belle Dame Sans Merci*, the same version, with " knight-at-arms," not " wretched wight," which Keats quotes with such humorous notes in his letter of 28th April, 1819, to George and Georgiana Keats. Leigh Hunt in the *Indicator*, May, 1820, published the " wretched wight " version, which, though probably the revised second version, is judged inferior by most critics.

Page 7. " To us as to the ancient Irish, the half-said thing is dearest." See Kuno Meyer's *Ancient Irish Poetry :* Introduction, and Study VIII of this volume.

Page 10. " Certainly I must confesse my own barbarousnes, I never heard the olde song of *Percy and Duglas*, that I found not my heart mooved more than with a Trumpet : and yet it is sung but by some blinde Crouder, with no rougher voyce, then rude stile : which being so evill aparrelled in the dust and cobwebbes of that uncivill age, what would it worke trymmed in the gorgeous eloquence of *Pindar* ? "—Sir Philip Sidney : *An Apologie for Poetrie*.

For two essays by Addison on *Popular Poetry : The Ballad of Chevy Chase*, see *Spectator*, Nos. 70 and 74.

Page 11. Examples of the absolute construction with " and " are found as early as Chaucer :

> " What couthe a stourdy housebonde more devyse,
> To prove hir wyfhode and her stedfastnesse,
> And he contynuyng ever in stourdynesse."
>
> *Clerkes Tale*, iv. 91.

There is another example in the same *Tale* at vi. 109.

Page 14. Quotation from *Poetry*. I use here and elsewhere what I find well said for my purpose, even when the thing is not daringly original.

Page 17.
> " A terrible and splendid trust
> Heartens the host of Innisfail :"

first lines of a poem by Lionel Johnson.

> " The heritage to the race of kings :"

first line of Mr. Joseph Plunkett's poem *Our Heritage*.

> " I saw thee arise
> With the lure of God in thine eyes :"

from *Banba*, by Thomas Boyd.

Poetry of Irish Opposition and Revolt is Chapter 12, Volume iv of Brandes' *Main Currents*.

Eamonn an Chnuic, Druimfhionn Donn Dilis and most of the other Irish and Anglo-Irish poems referred to in the text will be found in translation or in the original (English) among the *Poems of the Irish Mode* at the end of the book.

Page 19. The greater works of St. John of the Cross are *The Ascent of Mount Carmel, The Obscure Night of the Soul, A Spiritual Canticle between the Soul and Christ, The Living Flame of Love*. These consist of mystical poems with explanations. He has left besides seventeen poems without commentary.

Page 23. " The life and ways of the Gael." The Gael largely assimilated the old Danes and the Normans, who became *ipsis Hibernis Hiberniores*.

Page 25. " Certain Irishmen . . . expressed English or European life." These are here regarded altogether from the Gaelic standpoint. From the English point of view they seem to form a strong group, typical and expressive of Irish dissent and divergence. The term " Hiberno-English," recently coming into use, might be applied to these to distinguish them from those whose immediate inspiration is Irish.

Among the Hiberno-English writers represented in the first volume of the *Cabinet of Irish Literature* are Sir John Denham, Richard Flecknoe, Wentworth Dillon Earl of Roscommon, George Farquahar, Thomas Parnell, William Congreve. In the same work will be found accounts of some of the Irish writers who remained at home in body only.

. Page 26. " George Darley's reference to Irish history, his use of clan names." For instance, in *The Flight of the Forlorn : A Romantic Ballad Founded on the History of Ireland*, he has " Shan-avon " for Shannon, " Hi-dallan " as the name of an individual, and stanzas like this, full of errors :

> " Clan Tir-oen ! Clan Tir-conel !
> Atha's royal sept of Connacht !
> Desmond red ! and dark O'Donel !
> Fierce O'More ! and stout Mac Donacht ! "

" Curran's Irish phrases." One of his best known poems has these lines :

> " Thou gem of the west, the world's *cushla ma chree !* "
>
> .   .   .   .
>
> " Thy friendship is seen in the moment of danger
> And the wanderer is welcomed with *cushla ma chree.*"

Cuisle mo chroidhe means " pulse of my heart." Curran's lines are nonsensical. He must have known some Irish, but he probably regarded it as fair game for any use.

William Drennan's poems. Compare, for instance, the first stanzas of his two best known poems : *When Eire first Rose from the Dark-swelling Flood* and the *Wake of William Orr*. Nothing in Anglo-Irish verse surpasses the solemn simplicity of the second-named :

> " Write his merits on your mind—
> Morals pure and manners kind ;
> In his head as on a hill
> Virtue placed her citadel.

Why cut off in palmy youth ?
Truth he spoke, and acted truth—
' Countrymen, unite ! ' he cried,
And died—for what his Saviour died.

God of Peace and God of Love,
Let it not Thy vengeance move !
Let it not Thy lightnings draw—
A Nation guillotined by law !

.   .   .   .   .

Here we watch our brother's sleep ;
Watch with us, but do not weep ;
Watch with us through dead of night,
But expect the morning light."

Page 27. Charles MacLaughlin, who changed his name
to Macklin, was born in 1690 and died in 1797. He became
one of the greatest of English actors. He returned to Ireland
on more than one occasion, but finally died in England, where
he had played at Drury Lane chiefly, up to almost his hun-
dredth year. " This was the Jew that Shakespeare drew," in
Shylock. The plays of his that seem to us of most interest
are the *True-Born Scotchman* and *Love à la Mode*. The Theatre
of Ireland revived some years ago *The Irish Fine Lady*, under
the title of *The True-born Irishman*.

Page 28. *English as We Speak it in Ireland* is the title of an
interesting book by the late Doctor P. W. Joyce.

Page 33. For Carleton's letter from London see Mr. D. J.
O'Donoghue's Introduction to *The Black Prophet* (Laurence
and Bullen).

Page 34. " The function of the conventional word-order."
In English, since the decay of inflexions, word-order has the
function of making clear the meaning. In Old English the order
of words was nearly as free as that of Latin.   (See Leon Kellner:
Historical Outlines of English Syntax § 480.)   But yet modern
diction is not the only possible or the best.   " Modern syntax,
fettered by logic, is artificial, the result of literary tradition, and
therefore far from being a true mirror of what is going on
in the mind." (Ibid § 9.). Tennyson's line, " Flashed all their
sabres bare," follows the right order and is better than " All
their bare sabres flashed." Naturalness is, of course, another

matter, and my remarks here are no contradiction to what I
say at page 139 and elsewhere in this volume.

Page 40. The stock example of Alfred's style is his Preface
to the West Saxon version of the *Cura Pastoralis* of Gregory
the Great. It will be found in most Anglo-Saxon Readers
(for instance in Sweet's), in some anthologies of English Prose
and in such books as Kellner's *English Syntax*, cited elsewhere
in these Notes and recommended here for reference in connection with the development of syntax. An interesting book
more easily accessible (Kellner, has been out of print for some
time) is Sweet's Temple Primer : *The History of Language*.
Most books on the growth and structure of the English
Language give many examples of words that have come in
from history and of the puns and the blunders that have been
ennobled—words like " nap," the card-game, from Napoleon's
way of war, " tory " and " boycott " from Irish ways of
war. " Derring-do," a noun, is Spenser's misinterpretation
of Chaucer's verb in the line " In dorrying dōn that longeth
to a knyght." (In daring to do what belongeth to a knight.)
In looking at a dictionary now for confirmation of this reference
I find, before " derring-do " : " derrick, n. contrivance for
moving or hoisting heavy weights . . . . (obs. senses,
hangman, gallows, from name of hangman c. 1600)." After
" derring-do " comes " derringer, n. small-bore pistol (U.S.
inventor's name)."

Page 43. A few additional examples : *He went into fits of
laughter* for *He laughed loudly. What's on you ? They are
after killing the little dog on me*, (for *my little dog*). *I was not
going in under the table, and if I was itself, hadn't I the floor
swept ?* These forms are all used in Anglo-Irish.

Page 50. See W. B. Yeats' *Poems* (1912 edition) : Glossary
and Notes.

Page 51. *Ingin Ni Murachu*. The correct Irish form would
be *Inghean Ui Mhurchadha*. If Mr. Stephens spelled it *Inyan
ee Vurachu*, he would have been near the right. *Inghin* is the
dative or prepositional case of *Inghean* (daughter). " *Ni*, in-
declinable, used in *O* surnames of females . . . it is an
abbreviation of *Ni Ui* (from *Inghean Ui*)." (Dineen's Dictionary). *Murachu* (*Murchadha*) has not its initial consonant
aspirated as it should have. The cases in the correct Irish

Q

form are, nominative, genitive, genitive : Daughter of the descendant (grandson) of *Murchadh*, Daughter of O'Murrough.

Page 53. I have written on the metre of Ernest Dowson's poem in *Thomas Campion and the Art of English Poetry.*

Page 60. Lionel Johnson. Writing as I am of literature rather than of poets, I have not been able to do honour due to some Irish writers who go without that honour. Lionel Johnson was a great poet, different from the others of greatest name in this book, but not surpassed in his art by any. His lyrics are deliberate, builded, balanced, sonorous, full of dignity, but not the less spontaneous, not the less the creatures of a passionate art than those of fine careless rapture, not the less winged for other rapture and eyed for vision and for tears. To know fine poetry, read his long poem *Ireland.* I take a stanza at random :

" Nay ! we insult thee not with tears, although
With thee we sorrow : not as for one dead
We mourn for one in the cold earth laid low.
Still is the crown upon thy sovereign head,
Still is the sceptre within thy strong hand,
        Still is the kingdom thine :
The armies of thy sons on thy command
Wait, and thy starry eyes through darkness shine.
Tears for the dear and dead ! For thee, *All hail !*
        Unconquered Inisfail !
Tears for the lost : thou livest, O divine ! "

Read a poem on a subject that has been a net of poor prose to many poets, *Ninety-Eight :*

" *Who fears to speak of Ninety-Eight ?*
He, who despairs of Ireland still :
Whose paltry soul finds nothing great
In honest failure : he, whose will
Feeble and faint in days of gloom,
Takes old defeat for final doom.

.   .   .   .   .   .

Who fears to speak of Ninety-Eight ?
The renegade who sells his trust :
Whose love has rottened into hate
Whose hopes have withered into dust :
He who denies, and deems it mad,
The faith his nobler boyhood had."

Page 61. Mr. Clement Shorter is set down with the " men of law " by a mistake, which I regret. His edition of Emily Brontë's *Complete Poems* (1910) contains one hundred and thirty-eight new pieces, including the poem I quote. Except that three stanzas which seem incongruous are printed with it, no fault can be found with his editing of this, or, to my knowledge, of the others.

Page 62. Padraic O Prunta, spelled Padruig ua Pronntuidh in a MSS. volume in Irish written by him in 1763, now in the possession of Douglas Hyde. See *The Brontës* by Clement Shorter, vol. i., p. 23.

Page 63. For a popular account of the work of O'Donovan, O'Curry and Petrie, see *A Group of Nation Builders* by Rev. P. M. MacSweeney, M.A., Professor of English at Maynooth College, published by the Catholic Truth Society of Ireland.

Pages 64 *et seq.* On quantitive and accentual verse and other technical matters the author has written fully in his book on English prosody : *Thomas Campion and the Art of English Poetry.*

Page 65. *Accent and Rhythm explained by the Law of Monopressure,* published anonymously in 1888.

Page 69. In an admirable passage of the Introduction to his Selection of Spenser's Poems (The Golden Poet's Series : Jack) Mr. Yeats has shown the difference between the " marching rhythms, that once delighted more than expedient hearts " and the varied and troubled rhythms of a poetry that has " learned ecstasy from Smart in his mad cell, and from Blake, who made joyous little songs out of almost unintelligible visions, and from Keats, who sang of a beauty so wholly preoccupied with itself that its contemplation is a kind of lingering trance." He takes as example of this vaguely suggestive poetry a stanza of Shelley's *Laon and Cynthia,* which is in the Spenserian stanza ; and shows that the lines which are in Spenser like bars of gold thrown ringing one upon another, are in Shelley's poem broken capriciously. Spenser's verse rushes, as he says, to some preordained thought with that marching rhythm ; in Shelley's " the meaning is an inspiration of the indolent muses, for it wanders hither and thither at the beckoning of fancy." Rhythms do express emotions, and mingled rhythms express mingled emotions, in verse as in music.

Page 72.   *Deibhidhe* is one of the forms of Irish *dán díreach* or straight verse.   For a sample see text page 78.   It is impossible here to explain the technicalities of the *dán díreach*. Students are referred to Meyer's *Primer of Irish Metrics.* " The ancient pitch." That even the Romans marked pitch in their copies of poems is known from the fact that in the earliest codex of Virgil's works, a manuscript of the fourth century, in the Laurentian Library at Florence, are neumes as guides to the reciter.   Neumes, derived from the Greek accents, were used to represent the degrees of the scale.

Page 76.   Having quoted so much of *O'Hussey's Ode* here I omit the poem from the *Poems of the Irish Mode* at the end of the book, though it is one of the finest examples of the Mode.

Page 77.   I do not know that I should call the inversion " candles three " a forced phrase.   It is entirely justified and it is not at all of the same order as :

    " What will ye more of your guest and sometime friend ? "

At all events, in the matter of word-order poetry has other rights.   See page 34, and note thereon.

Page 79.   My keeping of the incorrect spellings of Irish words in the titles of poems, *Lene* for *Léin, Pastheen* for *Páistin,* must seem inconsistent with my claim for justice to Irish.   I do not, however, feel myself justified in altering an author's constant spelling of a title, though I am willing to correct his spelling of Irish words which have not assumed pseudo-English forms.

Page 81.   " Three things through love I see." From a translation of an Irish poem, *Taid na realta 'na seasamh ar an aer.*

Page 83.   See note to page 72, *Deibhidhe.*

Page 96.   " The Old Days of ' Unknowing ' in the fourteenth century."   The fourteenth century is one of the golden ages of Mysticism.   In England it produced *The Cloud of Unknowing* and other profound works.   So well were mystical works appreciated at the time that when a translation (*Dionise Hid Divinite*) of a work of Dionysius the Areopagite, was made, probably by the same author as *The Cloud of Unknowing,* it " ran across England like deere."   See Appendix to *Mysticism* by Evelyn Underhill (Methuen).   For a discussion of the language of the mystics, see the same work.   " No direct description of spiritual experience is or can be possible to man. It must always be symbolic, allusive, oblique : always suggest, but never tell, the truth." This itself suggests, but does not tell, the truth. That the words of a living language may have double use is certain. " In Chinese poetry," says Ernest Fellonosa, " every character has at least two shades of meaning, its natural and its spiritual,—or the image and its metaphorical range." (*Epochs of Chinese and Japanese Art.*)

Page 98. The passage by Lord Dunsany is from *The Gods of Pegana.*

Page 100 (footnote). Coventry Patmore to Francis Thompson. See Everard Meynell's *Life of Francis Thompson*, page 221. Patmore learned his lesson from Father Gerard Hopkins, himself a rare and to some of us an exquisite poet. He sent the priest his book of mystical poems, *Sponsa Dei*, in manuscript, and on receiving it back with the simple comment " This is telling secrets," burnt it. This I have from Father George O'Neill, S.J., M.A., Professor of English Language at University College, Dublin, who knew Father Hopkins here, and still has some unpublished music composed by him. Patmore has a single poem (published) entitled *Sponsa Dei.*

Page 102. Ronsard. The reference, of course, is to the famous *Sonnets pour Hélène.*

Page 103. A translation of " that untranslateable *Eamonn an Chnuic* " will be found on page 197. Judging from the attempts of Mangan and others, and from my own failure before to make anything like an adequate version, I wrote this sentence in the text. Since, in making my selection of Poems of the Irish Mode, I have, I hope, disproved it. As in the case of *Is Truagh gan Mise i Sasana*, page 150, I have omitted stanzas which I believe to be mere accretions to the true poem.

Page 105. *Urbanitas, curiosa felicitas, ego postera crescam laude recens,* " marvellous boy," " sleepless soul." " Criticism disdains to chase a school boy to his common places." Doctor Johnson : *Life of the English Poets : Thomas Gray.*

Page 108. Dr. Sigerson : See Introduction *Bards of the Gael and Gall.*

Page 111. John Eglinton. In his book of literary criticism *Pebbles from a Brook* (published at Kilkenny by Standish

O'Grady in 1901) and in the earlier *Literary Ideals in Ireland*
(*Daily Express* Office, Dublin, and Fisher Unwin, London,
1899) to which he contributed with W. B. Yeats, Æ, and the
late William Larminie, readers will find (if they can find the
books) interesting discussions of many of my subjects. It is
a pity that John Eglinton has not collected his critical studies.

Page 113. " The Golden Age of Irish Civilization." Ireland
was then indeed an island of Saints and Scholars. The Science
of the Saints was known and revered as it never has been
since in any whole nation.

Page 114. *Duanaire Finn* is the 1908 volume of the Irish
Texts Society.
    The Ulidian Cycle includes the great *Tain Bo Cuailnge* with
its attendant tales, among them the Deirdre Saga (*Oidhe
Chloinne Uisnigh* : The Fate of the Sons of Uisnech). The
Fenian Cycle is that of Finn and the Fiana (generally now
spelt Fianna) of the great poet Oisìn (son of Finn and father of
Oscar), of Diarmuid Donn and Grainne.

Page 118. The Standish O'Grady referred to is Standish
James, author of *The Bardic History of Ireland, The Coming
of Cuculain* and other romantic retellings of Irish story,
not Standish Hayes, of the *Silva Gadelica* and of the *Catalogue of
the Irish MSS. in the British Museum,* the most wonderful
catalogue ever made, being a great work in itself.   Standish
Hayes edited his first Irish text, *The Pursuit of Diarmuid and
Gráinne* in 1855, and died the 18th October, 1915, two days
before I wrote these words. Standish James still walks the
earth. I saw him do it this morning. " Years ago," wrote
Æ in the *United Irishman*, discussing a statement of O'Grady's
in his *All Ireland Review,* " years ago, in the adventurous youth
of his mind, Standish O'Grady found the Gaelic tradition like
an antiquated dún with the doors barred. Listening, he heard
from within the hum of an immense chivalry, and he opened
the doors and the wild riders went forth to work their will . . .
The wild riders have gone forth, and their labours in the human
mind are only beginning. They will do their deeds over again,
and now they will act through many men and speak through
many voices."

Page 123. Matthew Arnold's " touchstones " will be found
in the General Introduction to *The English Poets*, edited by
T. H. Ward (first published 1880). The Introduction is re-

published as the first of *Essays in Criticism*, second series (*The Study of Poetry*).

I sing of a maiden : " makeless," matchless ; " ches, ' chose ; " al so," as.

Page 124. For the utterly uninitiated (these notes in general are for the uninitiated) I must explain that An Craoibhín Aoibhin is the poet name of Douglas Hyde. It means The Pleasant Little Branch.

Page 126. *Domfarcai.* This little poem was discovered on the margin of one of the ancient manuscripts of St. Gall by Cavaliere Nigra. " While translating these verses," wrote the discoverer, " I love to imagine the poor monk who, more than a thousand years ago, was copying the manuscript and, taken off for a moment by the song of the blackbird, saw through the casement of his cell the green crown of woods which surrounded his monastery in Ulster or in Connacht ; and having heard the quick trilling of the bird, he wrote these verses and returned more lightly to his interrupted labours." See *Bards of the Gael and Gall*, Introduction.

Page 132. Many modern writers have attempted verse translations of the Lament, the best that I know is a fragment of eight lines quoted in an interesting little pamphlet *A Talk about Irish Literature* by *An Gae Bolga* (Dublin : Gill, 1907) :

" Ebb-tide to me,
   For with the ebbing sea my life runs out,
   Old age has caught and compassed me about,
   I mourn the glad youth passed away from me.

The flood-wave thine,
   Mine but the swift back-flowing ebb-tide's call.
   Out of my hand the ebb-tide carries all,
   Towards thee the flood-wave foams across the strand."

Page 134. Atkinson : *On Irish Metric* (Dublin : Ponsonby, 1884.)

Page 139. Comparisons like those I institute between the diction of Wordsworth and of the Anglo-Irish poets are generally unfair, as being of unlikes. Mine is not so ; the poems compared are similar in situation.

Page 143. The lovely harp in the Fenian lay had three strings, a string of silver, a string of bright brass, and a string of iron whole. The names of the strings were *Geantarghléas*, *Goltarghléas*, *Suantarghléas*, the string of laughter, the string of sorrow, the string of slumber. Padraic MacPiarais has two of these string's to his harp. For an account of the three see *Duanaire Finn* xvii.

Page 153. This same passage from *Séadna* is translated in *A Talk about Irish Literature* referred to in a previous note.

Page 164. Father Dineen in his edition of Eoghan Ruadh acknowledges that the poem has been attributed to *Maire Ni Sheadha*, but holds that the style is clearly Eoghan Ruadh's. The poem is *Maidean fhuar fhliuc ag eighre suas dam*.

Page 170. The *Aisling* describes a vision of Ireland. " A popular air," says Father Dineen, " was seized upon and wedded to a poetic vision of Erin as a virgin endowed with every grace of mind and with all loveliness, who appears to the poet and enthralls him with her beauty. The vision takes place either as he lies in bed, weary and oppressed, or as he saunters by some lonely river in melancholy mood, sorrowing over his country's ills. The poet, lost in wonderment at the queenly figure, reverently inquires of the virgin who she is, whether she is a human being or a goddess, whether Helen or Diana, or Deirdre or Cearnait, or the lady who brought over the Normans to our shores. The queen replies that she is none of these, but the spouse of the banished Stuart. Then she recounts her woes . . . There is the inevitable announcement of a speedy deliverance." No fewer than eighteen of the forty-four poems of Eoghan Ruadh collected by Father Dineen are *aislingi*, and the proportion in the work of others is as great. Like the Elizabethan sonnet in England, of which many thousands were published between Sidney and Shakespeare, the Irish *aisling* became a craze.

Dán díreach : See note to page 72.

" Schoolmen of condensed speech " is a mistranslation of a line in the Lament for the Bardic Schools by the great poet O'Gnive written in the beginning of the seventeenth century. The two words at the end of the first line of :

> *Ni clos sgoluidhe, sgeal tinn,*
> *D'Uibh nDalaigh na d'Uibh nUiginn.*

were taken to be *sgeil teinn*; so instead of " There are not (heard) scholars, a sore tale ! of the O'Dalys or of the

O'Higgins ", it was read " There are no schoolmen of condensed speech, etc."

Page 177. The list of poets here is not, of course, intended to be complete, but some omissions and the inclusion of some of those mentioned may seem strange, even in view of the limitations I have set. I shall deal with a few typical cases. Dr. John Todhunter (born 1839), an admirable poet, has written some poems of this mode. *Aghadoe* is in most of the anthologies :

("I walked to Mallow town from Aghadoe, Aghadoe,
Brought his head from the gaol's gate to Aghadoe,
Then I covered him with fern, and I piled on him the cairn.
Like an Irish king he sleeps in Aghadoe.")

Yet, living, as he has been, out of Ireland for many years, he is unknown to the present generation, as an influence nothing like Dr. Sigerson, for instance, even though he too has translated many of the ancient Irish poems.

T. W. Rolleston who has done much Irish work, I include principally for the value of his beautiful version of O'Gillan's poem *The Dead at Clonmacnois :*

—(" In a quiet water'd land, a land of roses,
Stands Saint Kieran's city fair ;
And the warriors of Erin in their famous generations
Slumber there.

.   .   .   .   .   .

Many and many a son of Conn the Hundred-Fighter
In the red earth lies at rest ;
Many a blue eye of Clan Colman the turf covers
Many a swan-white breast.")

Thomas Boyd, of whom we have heard nothing since the publication of his *Poems* in 1906 (Dublin : Gill), seems to me a poet sure to return and attain power. The twenty-five poems collected and published by Mr. O'Donoghue in the volume mentioned are all Irish, though of many modes. No one can read the *Leanan Sidhe* or *An Donn Cuailgne* without seeing a poet in them ; and they are not better than others in the book.

The work of Ethna Carbery is not as fine as that of Thomas Boyd, though some of her historical ballads will live:

(" I am Brian Boy Magee—
My father was Eoghan Ban—
I was wakened from happy dreams
By the shouts of my startled clan ;
And I saw through the leaping glare
That marked where our homestead stood
My mother swing by her hair
And my brothers lie in their blood . . .")

It is not of the Irish Mode, at all events ; it is ended (more's
the pity), and it has not shed seeds. So with the work
of others of whom I have made no mention in the text, It is
not a glory of this Mode now and it does not seem to me destined
for a better fortune. It is possible, of course, that I may have
forgotten some writer of real power. Throughout I have
had to depend mostly on my own reading and memory.
No literary movement of equal importance has received so
little notice from critics and historians, though the elder writers
of the present time have had a world-wide vogue for years
now.

Page 178. Poems of the Irish Mode. The great majority
of these poems are songs with very beautiful old Irish airs.
Almost all the Translations are so, and of course all the Ballads.
I should print with the Translations the original Irish poems,
but that I think it well to send students of Irish to the original
sources. To print them for others would be useless. If any
readers of these versions are prompted to begin their study of
Irish by a study of these originals, I would refer them to the
six penny booklets, *Ceol Sidhe*, published by the Irish Book
Company, Dublin. Mangan's *Poets and Poetry of Munster*
(Duffy) and Edward Walsh's *Irish Popular Songs* (Gill) give
Irish and English on opposite pages.

Page 182. Pastheen Finn. *An Paistin Fionn* means the
fair haired child, not brown girl sweet. Ferguson takes other
liberties with his original, but in general reproduces the rhythm
and effect of the song excellently.

Page 186. The unsigned poems and verse translations
here and through the book are the author's own.
Pearl of the White Breast is perhaps the least satisfactory
translation used here, as it does not turn into beautiful poetry,
and as it needs to a degree its air to set' it in this mode ; yet
as it is a faithful version, and by Petrie, I have let it stand.

Page 187. Flavell's name is written also Lavelle. George Fox was an early friend of Ferguson's. He left Ireland and was lost sight of by the poet, who long after, in 1880, dedicated his poems to him. Lady Ferguson, in her *Life* of her husband says that Ferguson was the writer of this translation, but that as it had been attributed to Fox, who had helped him with it, he refused later to claim it. All editors respect Ferguson's generosity with their right hands, but add a note like this with their left. The original reads to one like a poor translation into unidiomatic Irish. But it is in Hardiman's book, published in 1831, long before this version appeared, so it must be all right. Such wrong may a poet suffer at the hands of a translator !

Page 192. In a note to his edition of Mangan's Poems, Mr. D. J. O'Donoghue, generally most accurate of commentators, says that *A Farewell to Patrick Sarsfield* only distantly resembles the original. Except that it is not a complete translation, omitting some stanzas, it is wonderfully close to the Irish poem. Students can compare the version with the original in *The Poets and Poetry of Munster* (Dublin : Duffy).

Page 196. " William Heffernan, more usually called *Uilliam Dall* or Blind William, a native of Shronehill in Co. Tipperary, was born blind, and spent the greater part of his life, a poor houseless wanderer, subsisting upon the bounty of others." (Edward Walsh). He lived in the first half of the eighteenth century. His poems have never been collected.

Pages 197 and 198. *Eamonn an Chnuic* and *Druimfhionn Donn Dilis* are both in the form of dialogue, the former between Ireland and the Rapparee (though with its long tail of verses it assumed the form of an ordinary love poem), the latter between the Stuart and Ireland, the white-backed, brown, true, silk of the kine.

It will be noticed that assonance of final syllables in the original (*cnuic, fliuch*) is represented in the translation by rime, assonance of penultimates (*deanach, gaolta*) by assonance.

Page 199. Mr. J. H. Lloyd, who discovered and published *An Bunan Buidhe* (The Yellow Bittern), has told me that he suppressed some inferior stanzas. These I have never known. Mr. Lloyd wrote of Cathal Buidhe in *Irisleabhar na Gaedhilge* on more than one occasion, and in his book, *Duanaire na Midhe*. The poem, the song of a drinker, is certainly symbolical. I have authority for my translation of *Hallai Chuinn* by " Constantine's halls."

Page 200. *The Song of Gladness.* The vision of the bees seems wonderful in the work of a poet blind from birth, till we find that Heffernan barely mentions a swarm without a chief, the rest being Mangan's. Critics who would reduce the themes of lyric poetry to a small number, and find them appearing independently in many languages might find interesting parallels to the last stanzas of this poem. As Mr. D. J. O'Donoghue has pointed out, Fanny Parnell's fine poem *After Death* practically repeats it. Edward Walsh has translated this, as most of the other poems done also by Mangan and Ferguson. His versions are more literal but in general inferior. He gives the original in his *Irish Popular Songs*.

Page 203. *Shule Aroon.* I have kept the title used in the broad-sheets and in all editions of this street song ; but have spelled correctly the Irish refrain. The translation is :

" Walk, walk, walk, my (secret) love !
Walk, so quiet, and walk so soft,
Walk to the door and elope with me,—
And may you go safe, my darling ! "

An Craoibhin Aoibhin (Douglas Hyde) has an Irish version of this song which some day may be translated into English verse of the Irish Mode and so send this, like the Irish heroes in Æ's phrase, to do its deeds again and speak through many voices. To start it, I translate in prose the first verse of Dr. Hyde's version :

" O pleasant, handsome, youthful boy !
Wide was your heart, sweet was your kiss.
I wish that I were yours for life,—
And may you go safe, my darling !
Walk, walk, walk, my love !
There's no cure to get but the cure of death.
Since you have left me, poor is my case—
And may you go safe, my darling ! "

Page 204. *The Croppy Boy.* This is one of several versions of this famous ballad. It is chosen by me as being more interesting metrically than the others. The variant nearest to it, used by Padraic Colum in his *Broad-sheet Ballads* (Dublin :

Maunsel) has obviously been worked over. The second line becomes :

"When the small birds tune and the thrushes sing,"

The second stanza :

"It was early, early, on Tuesday night
When the yeoman cavalry gave me a fright,
To my misfortune and sad downfall
I was taken prisoner by Lord Cornwall."

On the other hand I am sorry to miss the two stanzas that take the place of the second last of this version :

"I choose the black and I choose the blue,
I forsook the red and orange too,
I did forsake them and did them deny,
And I'll wear the green like a Croppy Boy.

Farewell, father, and mother too,
And sister Mary, I have none but you ;
And for my brother, he's all alone,
He's pointing pikes on the grinding stone."

Of course Carroll Malone's version is practically a different poem. Though it is now more commonly sung, it is full of absurdities : "a vested priest," "*Nomine Dei*, the youth begins," and then the whole confession. Perhaps its preference is due to the two fine lines :

"I bear no hate against living thing,
But I love my country above my king."

Page 205. The Librarian of University College, Dublin, Mr. D. J. O'Donoghue, referred to frequently above, who knows more about Anglo-Irish literary history and publications than anyone else, has told me that this version of *The Streams of Bunclody* is a redaction by Halliday Sparling, editor of *Irish Minstrelsy* (Canterbury Poets Series) made from several variants. Readers will acknowledge that it has been well made. The lovely precision of "proceed," three stanzas from the end, and the wistful rambling of the closing line, might have been spoiled by a hand less true.

Page 208. I defy the malediction of Sam Lover against editors who omit the stanza added to *The Groves of Blarney* by Father Prout. Readers who are afraid to share my fate and think it their duty to read it, will find it in Prout's *Reliques*, or in any of the collections of the timid editors.

Page 209. Original Poems. I have to thank Alice Furlong, Seumas O'Sullivan and Joseph Plunkett for permission to use poems of theirs which they were able to give me without asking the permission of publishers. I decided when making this selection not to ask for copyright poems. Now that I am come to the end of my work, I am half tempted to regret not having broken my rule in some instances in order to secure other good poems which would introduce to my readers other authors with whose work I could not deal here. Again one instance must suffice for all. Dora Sigerson Shorter has written some of the best modern ballads, poems very distinctively Irish. Her work has a breath of romance all its own, that " breath of flowers " that she feared to leave behind in Ireland. Beautiful lyrics of hers, such as *Ireland* and *Can Doov Deelish*, may be read in the anthologies. I should like to have printed these and others. I comfort myself with the thought that my book may send some to her *Complete Poems*, where they will find them in a better atmosphere, as to the works of other good poets barely mentioned in this book. The published works of most of the Anglo-Irish poets of the time are within easy reach of everyone.

Page 210. *The Irish Peasant to his Mistress* is addressed to the Irish Catholic Church which suffered under the penal laws, not yet quite removed, persecution unparalleled.

BIBLIOGRAPHY.

In the text and in notes I have named many books, recommending some and censuring others. I can give here only a general guidance to readers for whom these Studies are an introduction to the literatures with which I deal. Books of reference in the subject are few, and, by comparison with those of other literatures, unsatisfactory. This study is still too new to have its histories and its appreciations complete. As there is really no knowing Anglo-Irish without some knowledge of Irish work, even at second hand, I would recommend readers to look into editions of Irish classics such as those of the Irish Texts Society (which has now published fourteen volumes) ; into the *Thesaurus Palaeohibernicus* of Whitley Stokes and John Strachan, the Introduction to the first volume and all the end of the second; into the *Silva Gadelica* of Standish Hayes O'Grady, and into numbers or volumes of *Eriu* (published by the School of Irish Learning, Dublin) *Gadelica* (Hodges, Figgis), *Celtic Review*, Scottish (London : Nutt), *Irisleabhar na Gaedhilge* (*The Gaelic Journal*) now dead, of the French *Revue Celtique* and the German *Irische Texte* and *Zeitschrift für Celtische Philologie*. The *Proceedings* of the old Ossianic Society are now, like many of these, hard to get, and, like them, fascinating. To mention editions and translations of individual classics, even of the *Tain*, would draw me aside from the main track. In the second volume of *The Irish Review* (1912-1913), Doctor Osborn Bergin edited for the first time a series of very interesting early Modern Irish poems. In the first and third volumes, Mr. P. H. Pearse edited the beginning of an Irish Anthology, Lyric Poems and Poems of Irish Rebels. To many of us the great treasure-house of Irish poetry is still James Hardiman's *Irish Minstrelsy* in two volumes (published 1831). It is rivalled in our days by Douglas Hyde's *Love Songs of Connacht* and *Religious Songs of Connacht*. Doctor Sigerson's *Bards of the Gael and the Gall* (Unwin) and Eleanor Hull's *Poem Book of the Gael* (Chatto and Windus) do not give the originals like the others, but refer readers to the sources, as does Kuno Meyer's *Ancient Irish Poetry* (Constable) a book of prose versions. Latterly, of course, there has been a constant stream of editions of Gaelic Poetry and Prose, known to all students.

The histories of Gaelic Literature are Douglas Hyde's large *Literary History of Ireland* and small *Story of Early Gaelic Literature* (Unwin) and Eleanor Hull's *Text Book of Irish Literature* in two volumes (Gill). They have to be read with caution.

Of Anglo-Irish Anthologies I have written at some length in the text. The Introductions to the Brooke-Rolleston *Treasury of Irish Poetry* (1890) and to W. B. Yeats' *Book of Irish Verse* (1895) and the notes on the life and work of the poets in the former work, are good. Anthologies not mentioned in the text are the first of all. Charlotte Brooke's *Irish Poetry* (1789) and Halliday Sparling's useful little *Irish Minstrelsy* (Scott : Canterbury Poets).

Doctor P. W. Joyce's *English as we Speak it in Ireland* is published by Messrs. Gill, Dublin. Professor Mary Hayden and Professor Marcus Hartog contributed to the *Fortnightly Review*, April and May, 1909, a study, *The Irish Dialect of English*. For an interesting list of books on the subject see Maurice Bourgeois' *John Millington Synge and the Irish Theatre*, pages 223 and 224, footnote.

It is impossible here to add much to what has been written in Study V by way of guidance to Anglo-Irish prose. The works of the authors there mentioned form the main bulk of the literature that is fixed. In our days we have had a considerable dramatic literature, written by Edward Martyn, W. B. Yeats, J. M. Synge, Padraic Colum, Lady Gregory and by a host of other authors who cannot yet be definitely placed. Their works are published mostly by Messrs. Maunsel, Dublin. We have had a great body of stories, sketches and essays. Most of the poets are also writers of prose. The most characteristically Anglo-Irish are Douglas Hyde again, Padraic Colum again, whose uncollected short stories are better than anything of their kind that I know, William Boyle, Emily Lawless, Lady Hartley (May Laffan), Jane Barlow, Seamus MacManus, Miriam Alexander, Shan Bullock and William Buckley. James Stephens has attained a very great contemporary reputation and deserves it. The early works of the late Canon Sheehan are among the best Anglo-Irish novels. W. B. Yeats is as great a master of prose as of verse and

distinctively Irish, too, though his work, in the main critical
and philosophic, is far apart from that of all the others mentioned here. His *Complete Works* are published by A. H.
Bullen, Stratford-on-Avon.

All the poets that matter I hope I have mentioned in the
text or in notes. A few of some fame I have omitted because
I do not think their work good. The principal Dublin publishers of verse are Maunsel and Hodges, Figgis and Co.
The catalogues of these houses contain lists of the authors
and their works.

The best encyclopædias of the subject are *The Cabinet of Irish
Literature*, in four volumes (Gresham Publishing Company),
which can easily be got, and the far finer but rare *Irish Literature*, in ten volumes (Philadelphia : John D. Morris Company :
1904). In *Every Irishman's Library* the Talbot Press (Dublin)
is issuing a series of anthologies of verse and prose and
editions of masterpieces of Anglo-Irish literature. For the
rest, go to the compilations and editions of D. J. O'Donoghue :
The Poets of Ireland (Hodges, Figgis), his *Life* and complete
edition of Mangan, his complete works of Lover, his editions
of some works of Carleton. Father S. J. Brown has just published a large book of reference, *Ireland in Fiction*, an extension of his *Reader's Guide to Irish Fiction*. He has also made
a *Guide to Books on Ireland*. To end with what I began
and therewith to assuage the learned who have forgotten that
this Bibliography is not for them, I give the name of the
great list of Gaelic books : *Bibliography of Irish Philology
and of Printed Irish Literature*, made by R. I. Best and published by the National Library of Ireland.

INDEX.

This Index does not repeat the directions of the Table of Contents : it does not give references to the Poems of the Irish Mode. It gives references to Notes only when new names and new matter are introduced in these. Otherwise, references will be taken to include notes. It does not cover the Bibliography.

Date Due

Demco 38-297